Good Luck
and TIGHT LINES!

Good Luck
and TIGHT LINES!

R. G. Schmidt

Gulf Publishing Company
Houston, Texas

Good Luck and Tight Lines

A Sure-Fire Guide to
Florida's Inshore Fishing

Gulf Publishing Company
Book Division
P.O. Box 2608 □ Houston, Texas 77252-2608

10 9 8 7 6 5 4 3 2 1

Library of Congress Cataloging-in-Publication Data
Schmidt, R. G.
    Good luck and tight lines! : a sure-fire guide to Florida's inshore fishing / by R. G. Schmidt.
        p.   cm.
    Includes bibliographical references (p.   ) and index.
    ISBN 0-88415-158-1
    1. Saltwater fishing—Florida. I. Title.
SH483.S33   1996
799.1'09759'09146—dc20   95-46756
                                                              CIP

Contents

Preface

"Great," you may be thinking, "just what the world needs; another fishing book."

Well, maybe so, if the world wants to catch some fish in the shallow waters found off the coast of Florida and in its scenic backcountry.

Lord knows there are plenty of books that will tell you how to catch a specific type of fish. There's probably not a species considered good eating or just plain great sport that doesn't have a book written on how to catch it. That includes the fish available in inshore Florida. So, even assuming you're going to fish there, why do you need this book, when you could just get the one on bonefish, the one on flounder, the one on redfish, the one on snook, the one on tarpon, the one on . . . ?

To be sure, those books will give you more specific, more detailed information on catching a given *particular* species of fish, and if you decide to specialize in catching those species, you should get a book written for anglers who do. This book, on the other hand, is written for those who don't yet know which species is going to become their favorite quarry, and for those whose time in Florida is going to be limited.

If you've recently moved to the Sunshine State, it will teach you how to catch fish—any kind of fish that's available where you are—in the shortest period of time. It doesn't matter if you have a boat or not, or if you prefer fishing from a bridge or walking the beaches. If it can be done in inshore Florida waters, it's in here.

Although bridge, pier, and surf fishing are covered in enough detail to make you successful in those endeavors, you'll note the emphasis in this book is on the shallow waters of Florida's lagoons, bays, and backwaters—what we in Florida call the "skinny water," sometimes only inches deep. That's because an amazing variety of tasty fish with superb fighting characteristics can be taken there on a wide variety of baits and lures.

If light tackle, catch-and-release sport fishing is your game, you may want to concentrate on a particular species, and once you've learned what fishing in skinny water is all about, you can specialize all you want. But because you're going to learn how to fish the shallows, why not catch something while you're at it?

Of course, catch-and-release may not be what you had in mind. Perhaps you're more interested in walking down to a local bridge, pier, or beach and supplementing the larder with some tasty whiting or pompano. You'll find the "how-to" in here.

Maybe you're not a new resident; maybe you're just a visitor. If so, welcome; this book was written with you in mind, and will help you enjoy your vacation even more. Residents have time to experiment and learn slowly; you don't. Your time in Florida is going to be limited, and it's our intent to save some of that time so you can use it to fish, instead of wasting it where you won't catch anything. If your trip to Florida is just in the planning stages, so much the better. Now you'll know what tackle to take, and what to expect when you get here.

Visitor or new resident, it's odds-on that Florida's inshore fishing is different from anything you've done before. I know this from having taught sport fishing classes to two types of students—those new to fishing and those who were experienced anglers who couldn't understand why the things they did "back home" didn't work for them here. I'll tell you as I told them: for the most part, forget the methods you used back home.

This kind of fishing is absolutely different. Not more difficult, but definitely different. The knots you've spent years learning will still come in handy, a hook is still a hook, and a swimming plug is still a swimming plug. Your tackle may even be suitable. That, however, is where the similarities between skinny water fishing and what you've done up to now end.

Acknowledgments

Few people know all there is to know about any type of fishing, and fewer still know everything about inshore fishing in Florida. I'm not one of those few. I've only been doing it about 30 of the 50-plus years I've been fishing, so I still have quite a bit to learn. Fortunately, I've been blessed, as a fringe benefit of my outdoor writing, by fishing and talking with many successful guides in all sections of the state. To say I've learned much from them is an understatement of the highest order: Roger Johnson of Inverness (who taught me more ways to carve a plastic jig tail to change the action than I would have thought possible); former Miami Dolphin lineman Terry Shaugnessy of Hackberry, Louisiana (a funny, funny man, and a great fishing guide); Paul Hawkins of St. Petersburg (I have to mention Paul, because when he won Top Guide in a Cotee Bait Company tournament, he publicly credited a lucky cast I made on the cruising redfish that put him in first place, but called it a "skillful" cast); Greg Koon and Gregg Gentile, both of Port St. Lucie; Mike Locklear, out of Homosassa, and many others, far too many to list. I thank them, one and all, and apologize to those I couldn't list.

In particular, I'd like to thank Captain Peter Greenan, of Sarasota, Florida. I've fished with Captain Peter more often than any other guide, for a number of reasons. When I have an assignment for a magazine article that requires photos I don't have on file, Captain Peter is the first one I call, and he's always come through. Need a photo of a ten-pound redfish being taken on a fly? "No problem, R. G., I have an open date on May 22; call me when you get in." How about tarpon in the hundred-pound range; I need some action photos, type of tackle unimportant. "No problem, R. G., I have . . . "

And so it goes, time after time. To Captain Greenan, a heartfelt "Thank you," and I'll collect my payment of Jack Daniel's on ice next time we're in Uncle Henry's.

In a manner of speaking, Captain Greenan is responsible for this book. I had the concept in my mind, had played around with a couple of chapters, but wasn't really serious about it. Then, on the CompuServe Information Service, I noticed a series of messages from people who had vacationed in Florida, expressing surprise there weren't any books that dealt with the basics of Florida inshore fishing. I began to think more seriously about writing the book. Shortly after that, I made a trip with Captain Pete.

We were fishing in Bull Bay, off Charlotte Harbor, and things weren't going as smoothly as they sometimes do. I needed action photos to accompany an article on catching snook in the shallows, but it had to be taken on a topwater plug. Because I don't believe in setup photos, we had to catch one that way; no catching it on a Cotee jig and replacing the lure for the photo shoot. The snook were being very camera shy, and I was fishing, too, so we'd have twice as much chance of a hookup.

During the course of the day, Captain Pete commented that at least "today's charter" didn't have to be told what to do, and said many of the people he guides resist adapting their usual methods to those that have been proven to produce in the backcountry; they want to fish "their way." He said if were a writer, he'd write a book about the basics of Florida fishing, and couldn't understand why nobody had.

That did it. That was the last nudge I needed, and I said "Okay Pete, I'll write one, but if I come up dry on any part of it, I'll be calling you."

"No problem, R. G., I have an open date on . . . "

I'd be remiss if I didn't also thank at least some of the manufacturers and their representatives who were so helpful with my research, in opening doors, in cutting corners and in supplying photos. In particular, Mike Walker of the Walker Agency, Steve Marusek of Cotee Bait Company, Eric Bachnik of L&S Bait Company and Nancy Hamilton and Laura Hilderbrand of the Lee County Visitor and Convention Bureau were of tremendous assistance, and the help of Victor Biggs of Uncle Henry's Marina in Boca Grande, right in the heart of some of Florida's best fishing, was invaluable.

Enough of that. It's time now to get on with learning about fishing the skinny water. I hope, and I expect, you will find this book both helpful and entertaining. If not, it's Captain Greenan's fault.

R. G. Schmidt
Cloverhill
Columbia County
Florida

Good Luck
and TIGHT LINES!

Introduction

Welcome to Florida. Or to fishing inshore waters. Or to fishing inshore waters in Florida. Pick one. Whichever case applies, you're obviously interested in learning about catching fish in the waters near Florida's shoreline, or its estuaries, marshes, mangrove islands, beaches or back country.

You've come to the right place, in more ways than one.

If you're looking for outstanding fishing done in unique ways, for truly great game fish under some of the finest conditions imaginable, Florida's the place to find it. If you need help because this is a different style of fishing than that to which you're accustomed, this book is the place to find that help.

It's a much-overused word, but Florida fishing, especially in the shallow inshore waters, truly is unique. In the United States, only certain marshy areas along our eastern coastlines and some states bordering the Gulf of Mexico offer anything close to it. Even then, there are differences. I remember fishing for small striped bass in the salt marshes of Long Island's Jamaica Bay back in the fifties, where we found them near the mouths of the creeks and cuts that wound through the marsh grasses.

I was a teenager then, and I often wonder if that great fishing for school bass still exists there in the shadow of what was then Idlewild Airport. There weren't many who fished that way for stripers; most fished around the bridges, especially at night. But a few of us knew those smaller bass worked the creek mouths even after daylight, and sometimes right through the day. What we were doing was revolutionary, made possible primarily by the introduction of a new type of reel from a guy named Mitchell; he called it a "spinning reel."

The open-faced spinning reel and the fiberglass rod together made it not just possible, but actually practical for the first time to toss small artificial lures at big fish and actually land them. Land the fish, not the lures. It was awesome, and that style of fishing imprinted itself permanently on my young self. I've never lost the excitement of seeing a big fish bust a topwater bait, especially in shallow water.

That was shallow water fishing, too, and some of the things I learned then I was able to apply when we moved to Florida. It was similar fishing in some ways, vastly different in others. Nowhere does that ability to use small lures and baits and light tackle translate into great fishing more than in the tropics and subtropics, especially in the shallow water coastlines.

One thing about shallow water is the only place a fish has to go is up or away from you. No diving into a deep hole to wait you out.

Florida's inshore waters are home to many species that have turned "going up" into an art form. Fish as small as one-pound ladyfish, as bullish as 15-pound snook, and as monstrous as 150-pound tarpon will all become airborne during a fight, as though to see what it is they've caught this time. What a thrill that is to see.

Of course, there are dangers in this going up business. More than once I've been left wondering how I'm going to recover my fly line, left hanging in a tree across a canal after a tarpon tore through the water's surface directly under an overhanging tree, crashing up and then down through its branches, leaving my line hopelessly entangled.

It wouldn't be so bad, if they didn't snicker as they left the area. Adding insult to injury is another specialty of Florida's inshore fish.

Of course, all the fish found inshore aren't part-time tree dwellers, nor even very acrobatic. There are redfish, for example, whose scientific name (according to an article I wrote, and I wouldn't lie) is *Pullumous mosthardus*. The redfish solution to being hooked is to go "over there." It doesn't much matter where "over there" is, either. From the perspective of a redfish, "there" is anyplace but "here," because "here" is where something has it by the mouth and is pulling it toward the funny looking monster fish floating on the surface.

So, because "here" isn't good, he goes "there." Preventing that is the angler's job, and it isn't often easy. Redfish don't jump or perform other acrobatic tricks. They'd never make the Olympic gym team. They'd be naturals, however, for the tug-of-war event.

Then there are snook. Crafty little rascals. They jump, especially the smaller ones, but that's just out of curiosity, to see, as I said earlier, what they've got now. Their main trick is to find a nearby piling, pier, or mangrove root, take a few turns around it with your line and sit there, as if to ask what your next move is. If that stunt fails, they have a weapon that would be illegal in most U.S. cities; razor-sharp plates at the bottom of their gill covers. One swipe across your line with those plates and he's off to get a beer. Incidentally, those gill plates will do a job on your hand, too, so be careful while unhooking a snook.

Everybody knows about tarpon. The Silver King, he's called. Monster prehistoric fish with primitive lungs, they have a couple of reasons for fighting near the surface and for jumping. First, of course, they want to get rid of that thing in their mouth. Additionally, they gulp air for a bit of extra energy. Couple their fighting ability with their very hard, bony mouth, and it's easy to see why most hooked tarpon aren't landed.

But these glamour fish aren't the only inhabitants of the inshore areas. There are flounder (summer flounder), many kinds of snapper, some grouper (although most grouper are found offshore in deep water), sheepshead, spotted sea trout, and many, many lesser-known species. All can be caught on hook and line (even, contrary to what you may have been told, mullet) and all will give a good account of themselves if you use the right tackle and don't simply overpower them. There are ladyfish (also called tenpounder, but I'll never know why; they don't get that big), jack crevalle, moonfish, lookdowns, whiting, Spanish mackerel, squirrelfish, bluefish, cobia, bonefish, permit, pompano, sharks of various kinds, and, of course, crabs, shrimp, oysters, and I'm running out of breath, so I'll stop there.

Many are excellent table fare, plenty are just great sport. Some are both. The variety of life found inshore is amazing, even if you exclude the numerous offshore species that spend their juvenile years inshore, then leave for larger and wider horizons, and the non-fish such as crabs, shrimp, scallops, oysters, porpoise, sea turtles, and manatees. By the way, those last three are all protected; don't mess with them.

Just about anything that swims in Florida's shallows can be caught on rod and reel. What you need to know to get started can be found in these pages. They comprise an accumulation of knowledge gained through thirty years of fishing in Florida. Some was learned the hard way, some stolen from unsuspecting professional fishing guides (as if there were really such a thing; guides are born suspicious) while researching newspaper or magazine articles, or passed on by those who took pity on me.

In choosing to fish Florida's "skinny water," you've made an excellent decision. I wish you good luck and tight lines. There's a real treat in store for you.

Chapter 1

What Makes Florida Fishing Unique?

The state of Florida is itself a migrant, which may be one of the reasons it's so receptive to new residents and to visitors from all over the world.

"As steady as the ground you walk on" is a relative statement. Compared with most things we encounter in everyday life, the ground is stable and unmoving. Geologically speaking, however, there's nothing stable about it, and I'm not referring to earthquakes or mud slides.

Seems the continents just won't stay put. They keep moving all over the face of the globe.

You may already know some of what follows, but I ask you to bear with me, as there is a point, and it has to do with fishing the inshore waters. I promise.

A cross section of the earth would show that it's not a solid mass, but is made up of a core surrounded by concentric layers of materials of varying densities. More like a baseball or golf ball than a ball bearing.

The top layer, consisting of the crust and the upper mantle, is the most solid, and is called the lithosphere. It ranges in thickness from 30 to 90 miles, and "floats" on the next level, called the asthenosphere, which is much hotter and softer; it is, in fact, molten.

If you examine water heating in an open pot on a range, you'll see currents being set up within the water as it heats. So it is with the asthenosphere, and these currents have an effect on the earth's crust.

The crust isn't one solid piece; it's made up of sections, or plates, irregular in shape and pattern, making the earth's surface a mosaic. These tectonic plates move about, drifting on the molten surface of the asthenosphere. The movement is undetectable for all practical purposes, being a matter of centimeters per year— about the same rate at which your toenails grow.

It's generally agreed within the scientific community that all earth's land masses were once one huge continent, which Those Who Name Things called "Pangaea." There's speculation as to the actual sequence of events, but a series of mergings and separations led eventually to the formation of the North American continent, following, about 700 million years ago, the "Grenville collision." You remember that one, I'm sure; made a heck of a bang.

Dependent on the relative speed of two colliding masses of land, one plate may be "subducted" (pushed below the other), or the two continents may, in shoving against one another, bulldoze up enormous amounts of rock. In the first case, volcanoes are usually formed; in the second, mountains. It was a series of such collisions that gave the North American continent its great mountain ranges, including the Appalachians, the Smokies, the Rocky Mountains, and, believe it or not, the hills of northern Florida. (An old Florida cracker saying claims "If it weren't for Georgia, Florida would have mountains.")

A theory with growing support holds that a collision between the continents Laurentia (North America), Baltica (northern Europe and parts of Scotland), and Gondwanaland (a huge super-continent comprising Africa, South America, and, possibly, what would later become England and southern Europe) pushed a part of North America known as "Avalon" a thousand miles to the north, creating in the process the Ouachita mountains, and the great curving sweep of the southern United States coast.

Now we're getting to the good part.

Further speculation, based on scientific measurements, indicates that a portion of Gondwanaland remained attached to North America when the continents rebounded. Holes drilled through the sediment layers of northern Florida have penetrated rock 350 to 450 million years old, which bear fossils of an African affinity. It would certainly seem that Gondwanaland, destined to give birth to Africa, first left a keepsake tacked onto the bottom of North America, closing the end of the circular coast and creating the Gulf of Mexico. I don't know why Those Who Name Things didn't call it the Gulf of Florida, or the Gulf of Louisiana, or Texas, or . . . Never mind.

Let's jump forward just a bit now, nearly 700 million years, to a period about 1.8 million years ago. Repeatedly, for 2 million years or so, glaciers had alternately covered the continents and retreated toward the poles. Each repetition of the cycle saw vast amounts of water alternately locked up in the glaciers and released into the oceans of the planet. As these cycles repeated, obviously, the sea level alternated between high and low extremes.

You've heard the expression "Having your ups-and-downs?" Florida's alternately been immersed in the ocean and exposed to the atmosphere so often residents ought to get free coffee at Dunkin' Donuts.

Each time the Florida peninsula has been covered by the seas, layers of sediment have been laid down, one atop the other. Much of this sediment is composed of shells from tiny marine animals. It's this accumulation of sediments that has given Florida its soils, and its native rocks. (Limestone and coquina limestone, frequently and incorrectly called coral.)

Gently sprinkling sediment into water creates a relatively smooth bottom, which is why most of the state is so flat. The highest point in mid-Florida is less than 300 feet above sea level, and only north of Ocala can anything remotely resembling hilly country be found. This flatness extends into the water, and is what makes the prolific plant and animal life in the inshore waters possible. Because the water is so uniformly shallow, large amounts of sunlight can penetrate to the bottom.

As with most rules, there are exceptions. In the northwest, the section known as the Panhandle, we find white, sandy beaches that quickly drop off to deep water. Here, you can fish in seventy feet of water and still see bathers on the beaches. The Atlantic coast also has some places that quickly drop off to deep water. For the most part, however, Florida's inshore waters are shallow, and it's those shallow waters, the "skinny water," with which we're concerned.

It was in the Pleistocene epoch, nearly 2 million years ago, that some of the rearrangements made in the area now known as the Caribbean took on new meaning. A combination of the most recent retreat of the glaciers and the warming effect of the currents established by the new positions taken by the continents was responsible for the climate that developed in Florida and resulted in what may have been the greatest proliferation of life forms in the history of the planet. Were it not for that Grenville Collision so long ago, and the multiple immersions, the shallow, warm inshore grounds—the skinny water—would not exist.

So, here we are, on a peninsula sticking out between what has become two separate bodies of water, forcing currents of warm water to go around us, with gently sloping continental shelves, for the most part, on both coasts. The shallow waters and deep sediments are ideal for the growth of marine grasses and specialized trees, which together comprise a nursery for a profusion of juvenile marine life found in few places on the planet.

We're doing our level best to destroy this nursery, but so far it's holding its own against us.

It may seem strange, but there's more marine life in the super cold arctic and antarctic waters than there is in the warm shallows of tropic and sub-tropic Florida. It's just a different kind of marine life. Those cold waters are saturated with microscopic life forms that most often simply drift with currents while waiting to be dined on by filter feeders such as whales.

It's the absence of all those copepods and other plankton that gives southern waters their amazing clarity. To oversimplify, the greater the clarity of the water, the lower the density of life in that water. That doesn't mean tropical waters are barren; in fact they are teeming with life. It just isn't, for the most part, microscopic.

Florida's unique construction affords the opportunity for the development of three major configurations, all of which are vital to the establishment of the type of fishery found here. There are salt marshes, "flats," and mangrove islands and shorelines. It would be difficult to say which of the three is more important, from the standpoint of a nursery.

In fact, a good argument could be put forth in defense of any of the three. By far the most extensive, and therefore the one you are most likely to encounter, are the flats areas. Flats are found in one form or another in every part of the state, from Fernandina Beach, down the coast, around the Keys and back up to the Panhandle. While you may have to travel to find mangroves or salt marshes, a grass or mud flat, or an oyster bar is never far away no matter where in Florida you are.

Barrier Islands

Before we get into flats, however, we need to first look at what are called "barrier islands." Barrier islands don't appear only in Florida; they occur all along the east and Gulf coasts of the continent. However, they are an important part of the ecology, and allow the development of, among other things, the flats that harbor so much of Florida's marine life. Fishing inshore Florida waters, you'll spend a good deal of time on or near barrier islands.

The easiest way to understand barrier islands is to keep in mind their name. They're named for what they do; provide a barrier between the mainland and the storms that build up offshore on a regular basis. If large enough, as on Florida's east coast, barrier islands create huge lagoons between themselves and the mainland. The misnamed Indian River is one such, and will be referred to herein by its proper name, the Indian River Lagoon. This barrier island, and the lagoon it creates, runs from north of Cape Canaveral all the way to Jupiter, over 150 miles.

It's important, if we are to understand the development and day-to-day workings of the flats, to also understand the manner in which barrier islands are supposed to "work," which is to say the way in which nature "designed" them. The first thing to understand is that they are not supposed to be permanently in place.

Let's ignore, for a moment, the way barrier islands have been mishandled on the east coast, and consider the way they should function, and do in many places on the Gulf coast. Just for fun, let's assume barrier islands do work as intended, and keep everything in the present tense. It will make for easier reading on your part, and save me a slew of "shoulds," "supposed tos" and "intendeds."

Protected from the waves of the ocean or the Gulf, the shallow waters of a barrier island lagoon build up a good layer of fertile muck. Coupled with the steady supply of sunlight that easily penetrates the clear shallow water, this encourages extensive areas of marine grasses. These grasses provide both food and shelter for myriad sea creatures, from many species of invertebrates, mollusks, and crustaceans to a variety of fishes. In many cases, only the juvenile stage is found in these lagoons, but in many others, a whole life can be spent there, with some time out spent offshore spawning.

Periodically, openings (called "inlets" on the east coast, "passes" on the Gulf side) occur in the barrier islands, allowing free exchange of gulf or ocean water on each tidal cycle. If a barrier island is very long (as is, for example, that part of Hutchinson Island in Martin and St. Lucie Counties), the tidal flow at the center (measured from each inlet) of the lagoon will be close to nonexistent. This causes an accumulation of detritus such as dead grasses, leaves from trees, etc. Eventually, the decaying of this vegetation will use up much of the oxygen in the water, making it unsuitable for the support of life. (This process is called "eutrophication.") In the meantime, the decayed "compost" sinks to the bottom, further enriching the "soil," as in every forest on earth.

It's obvious, then, that the center part of a large lagoon is in a constant state of dying, in the sense that it's steadily approaching the point where marine animals and fish will have to leave it. Fortunately, Ma Nature has things under control. (If left alone, and that's a mighty big "if," unfortunately.)

From time to time, major storms will break through barrier islands which, for the most part, are very narrow, for reasons we won't go into. Suffice it to say they are long and narrow, generally, and it's relatively easy for storm waves to broach barrier islands. Consequently, inlets or passes are alternately created and filled in. Broaching a barrier island and creating a new inlet allows ocean or gulf water, rich in oxygen, to replace the "dead" water far from the old inlet, and new marine growth quickly springs up in the rich bottom muck. The filling in of the old inlet now places that area far from replenishing water, and the cycle of growth and eutrophication starts anew in another section of the lagoon.

When man, in his infinite wisdom, alters things, it's usually the ecology that suffers. Using Hutchinson Island as an example again, we can see this plainly. Because there are now two "permanent" man-made inlets (Fort Pierce and St. Lucie) in the island, storm-driven waters find it easier to enter and leave the lagoon at those places, than to break through the island and create new inlets. Consequently, the area halfway between those two inlets (around Blind Creek and Big and Little Mud Creeks) is in pretty much a constant state of eutrophication.

Unfortunately, it's likely that it won't be until the inevitable major hurricane hits the area, and that island, that the lagoon will be flushed out properly again. From an ecological standpoint, this will be a good thing. It's tragic that human suffering and economic losses will accompany it, but the ecology has been chugging along this way for too many millenia to change just because we have decided barrier islands are nice places to live.

Causeways built by dredging sand and laying it down in a narrow strip across the lagoon in order to have a road from the mainland to the island exacerbate the situation by further restricting an already minimal tidal flow.

Inlets created naturally in these barrier islands tend to be relatively shallow, with notable exceptions such as Boca Grande Pass on the southwest coast, which has extensive rock and coral formations that create deeper waters. (It's in this deep water of the pass that most of the huge tarpon in the area are taken, generally by anglers drifting live baitfish in the depths.)

Shallow inlets and slow currents cause water coming in from the gulf or ocean to drop any sediment soon after entering the lagoons, and the deltas that build up are readily apparent from the air. Staying with Hutchinson Island, one can easily see the deltas from an old inlet, on the lagoon side near Jack Island State Park on the northern half of the island. Because St. Lucie Inlet is shallower and less protected than Fort Pierce Inlet, similar formations can be found north of St. Lucie Inlet, back toward Stuart.

Shallow, warm, sun-drenched, oxygen-rich water with light tidal currents over soft muck filled with nutrients; just what every gardener wants.

Okay, now we know how barrier islands and lagoons are formed, and why grass beds develop behind them, especially on the east coast of the state. On the west coast, where the Gulf of Mexico is so much shallower than is the Atlantic Ocean, grass flats also develop quite well without the assistance of barrier islands.

The Flats

Things seem to run in threes in Florida, and, sure enough, there are three very broad and basic categories of flats, defined primarily by what's found on them.

Most common is the *grass flat*. Frequently found at the edge of mangrove islands or the interior side of barrier islands, these grassy areas can be mere hundreds of feet long or can go on for miles. Grass flats are the backbone of Florida's fisheries, offering at the same time both prey and shelter from predators. Sometimes, you actually can have it both ways, contrary to the old adage.

Nearly everything that swims in Florida spends part or all of its juvenile life on grass flats, from shrimp and crabs to game fish, including many pelagic species. The grass offers food for vegetarians and hiding places for prey and predator alike. They are among the most productive marine areas on the planet, and make an excellent starting place in your search for sport fish.

Next we have smaller flats of mostly sand or mud, but whose distinguishing characteristics are the *oyster bars* found at the edges and sporadically on the surface of the flat proper. Sometimes a flat will have both grass and oysters, but the ones we're interested in here are strictly oyster flats. Much smaller than most grass flats, they are generally referred to as "bars" rather than flats, but either designation will work.

Finally there are the *mud flats,* which are just what you'd think; extensive shallows with sparse grass, a few oysters or neither. In south Florida, many of these flats consist of marl, a mixture of mud and broken pieces of shell, coral, and limestone. The mud flats are the least productive of all flats, as there's little there to attract or hold fish; neither food nor hiding place, with few exceptions. Don't always ignore them out of hand, however, as there are times when they will hold fish. The marl of the southern mud flats in particular holds many crabs and other animals that attract predators, and frequently even has extensive plant growth.

One word of caution. While wading is one of the more effective methods of fishing flats, it isn't generally recommended for marl flats. Marl bottom is frequently very soft; you can easily slip in past your knees with little or no warning. If you want to wade the marl bottom, use a cane or some sort of probe to check the bottom ahead of you. In some cases, marl bottom can be as firm as a grass flat, but it isn't something on which you can depend. In fact, using a probe is a good idea in a new area regardless of the type of bottom.

Good grass flats, defined as those likely to hold the largest number and variety of fish, are large, with three to four feet of water at high tide, and thick, healthy grass of several varieties. Such flats will attract and hold many small fish, crabs, snails, and other morsels for predators. This abundance of life will in turn attract not only predatory species of fish, but also many types of bird life, such as egrets, herons, ospreys, and pelicans, all of which can be seen actively feeding.

While most of these birds will go to roost in nearby trees at night, constant daytime feeding activity is a good sign. These birds are after the same food sought by flounders, redfish, snook, trout, tarpon and a veritable plethora of fish species. If you notice a particular area being regularly visited by wading and diving birds, it's a good bet you've found a grass flat worth your attention at the right stage of the tide. Feeding birds aren't a sure sign of gamefish, but at least you know the food supply is there for them.

While not technically grass flats per se, the west coast of Florida has extensive reaches of grass beds, especially the region from just north of Charlotte Harbor all the way to the Suwannee/Steinhatchee/Horseshoe Beach area. The gentle slope of the continental shelf at that point in the Gulf means that you can sometimes be out of sight of land and still have less than ten feet of water under the boat.

Six to ten feet of water, if it's clear enough, will still allow enough sunlight to penetrate for certain types of grass to flourish, and that grass will hold many of the same types of fish as do the grass flats along the shore. Although many of these beds are too far north for snook, both trout and redfish frequent them, along with cobia and several types of snapper. Those beds that are near ledges or rock formations will also hold some grouper, and Spanish mackerel, tarpon, and an occasional kingfish (king mackerel) will cruise through.

Oyster bars attract fish too, but not, as many believe, because the fish feed on the oysters. Although oysters are no doubt consumed by strong-mouthed fish such as black drum, which have pharyngeal teeth that can actually crush oyster shells, it's the small crabs and minnows found on the bars that attract predators. If you ever have the opportunity to watch an oyster harvester at work, pay particular attention when the oysters are first dumped onto the culling board. You'll see dozens of tiny crabs, shrimp and fish scurrying and flopping on the board. That's what the fish you seek are after, for the most part.

Finally, there are those apparently sterile mud flats, which hold more life than they appear to, mostly in the form of worms, clams and, in some cases, crabs, especially fiddler and ghost crabs. As was stated earlier, don't ignore them out of hand. Because there's little to distinguish one section of a mud flat from another, this is primarily sight fishing. There are often no holes, grass, or oysters to hold fish, and any that are on a mud flat are probably just cruising in the hope of catching a worm with his head out of the mud or a crab incautiously far from home.

Mangroves

The Seminole Indian word for mangroves translates loosely into "trees that walk in the water," and that's certainly what they appear to be doing. There are three types of mangrove tree in Florida (there's that Rule of Three, again), white, black, and red. All three are not found throughout the state, and each species has a different degree of liking for pure salt water. For our purposes, however, we can treat all three alike, because we aren't interested so much in the trees as in what it is they harbor. To fully appreciate that, we do need to know just a bit of their life cycle.

Mangroves start out as a roughly cigar-shaped seed that drops into the water from a parent tree. Infrequently, they stick in the mud and commence growing right at momma's feet. More often, they drift off on the tidal currents. Eventually, they'll wedge against the mud in some shallow area, put out a root as an anchor, and start growing.

Mangrove roots, as do those of cypress trees, serve several purposes. In the manner of the knees at the base of cypress trees, mangrove roots support the tree and brace it against storm winds and strong tides. The interlocking root system is extremely efficient at anchoring mud and sediment against tidal currents. Ironically, in fact, black mangrove trees are more efficient at holding back erosion than are most of the concrete or steel sea walls that replaced them.

Again as with cypress trees, some mangrove roots contain pneumatophores, openings through which oxygen can be taken, to compensate for the anaerobic nature of the mud in which they are growing. The net result of this complex above-ground portion of the mangrove's root system is a maze of crossing and interlocking branch-like roots that not only anchors sediment, but creates a multitude of hiding places for small fish, crabs, etc., and a home for barnacles and other permanently-housed crustaceans.

Mangrove root systems are crustacean condominiums, and although they do only limited advertising, have no difficulty attracting new residents. They share two things with the condominiums used by humans, however; they have a great view, but crime in the parking lots can be a major problem. Their alleys and passageways are populated by a rough crowd of homeless fish, cruising for a handout or an easy meal.

Barracuda, grouper, jacks, jewfish (small ones), redfish, sheepshead, snapper, trout, but most especially snook are well aware of these hiding places, and not only prowl them looking for food, but frequently hide there themselves, waiting to ambush an unsuspecting traveler like a panhandler at an automatic teller machine outside a halfway house. In the channels at the edges of the mangroves, tarpon cruise for a meal; the town bully, daring crabs, mullet, pinfish, and pigfish to come out and play.

On the highest tides, there can be enough water for a ten-pound fish (frequently, a foot is all it takes) many yards back into a mangrove system, but as the tide drops, the fish will move back out to the edges. In some cases there's enough water in a mangrove stand at every tidal stage to hold fish, while other areas will be sufficiently flooded only at high tide. Sometimes the fish will be holding too far back for your casts to reach them. No matter the stage of the tide, however, it's critical to get your lure or bait right up to the edge of the trees. A foot away isn't close enough. The predators are up inside the root system because that's where experience has taught them their food hangs out. That's where your bait needs to be.

Now that you understand how extensive these root systems are, and how far back they can go, you probably have a better appreciation for the need to get your lure in close. There are those who believe two or three feet away is close enough, but that's because they don't know as much as you now do about the extent of those root systems.

Here's a little story that illustrates not only that need, but also the size of the fish found in these shallow waters.

I was fishing out of Port of The Islands, on the southwest coast, near Marco Island, with guide Pete Greenan and fellow outdoor writer G. B. Knowles, in a Cotee Bait Co. fun "tournament." I flipped a jig into the mangrove roots at the edge of a little island in a small bay, where the water was eight or so inches deep. A snook came out of the tree roots and nailed the jig before it had moved a foot. We estimated its weight at six to seven pounds, and released it, but before we did we examined an old scar that appeared to be a healed wound from a boat propeller.

Shortly after that, we moved across the bay to try for some redfish in a couple of channels and, after an hour or so, had worked the shoreline almost back to the spot where I'd gotten the snook. Captain Greenan noticed what looked like a fish lying on an exposed mud bank. Wading ashore, he discovered it was the same snook, minus about six inches of its tail. The old scar identified it beyond any doubt. The fish was still alive, but wouldn't be for long so, even though Cotee tournaments are catch-and-release, we kept it.

Two points are illustrated here. First, a six- to seven-pound fish felt comfortable in less than a foot of water; second, something large enough—maybe a shark, maybe a porpoise, probably the latter—to chase, catch and bite off the tail of a snook that size was cruising around in a bay three feet deep at most, in the middle of the day.

The inshore waters of Florida hold an abundance of marine life more varied than you can imagine. Fortunately, you don't have to imagine it; you can experience it first hand by simply being observant. For a treat you'll remember the rest of your life, get out on the flats at night, with a powerful light. I simply hang a Coleman lantern from the shaft of my trolling motor, but there are handheld and floating lights that can be used, too. Shut off all power and simply drift across a flat at night, with the light shining through the water to the bottom.

You'll see small fish, crabs, shrimp, oysters, scallops, sea urchins, sea slugs, lobsters, and on and on. In addition, you'll see some surprisingly large flounder, redfish, snook, and trout, depending on where you are geographically. It will give you an insight into what's there that you can't ordinarily see, and will be an educational experience you'll never forget. If you have children, it's a super way to introduce them to Florida's marine environment. Not all human uses of the skinny water involve consumption, and drifting the flats at night is one of the finest non-consumptive ways to enjoy that environment you'll ever find. If it's at all possible for you to do this, don't miss the opportunity.

One last thing about the Florida ecology. Nearly surrounded by water, and located so far south, Florida tends to be hot and humid. I know, a real news bulletin. But it's important to keep in mind for two reasons. First, be sure you are protected adequately from the sun. Check with your doctor or pharmacist, and be certain you're using a sun screen of the proper rating, and find some shade from time to time. Don't be lulled by a soft breeze into becoming both overheated and sunburned.

Second, the heat in the tropics and sub-tropics causes a constant evaporation of water from the Gulf and from the Atlantic. Rising into the cooler layers of the atmosphere, this vapor creates huge thunderstorms that can spring up quite unexpectedly, especially during the rainy season, which runs roughly from June through November. Frequently, these storms form squall lines that can be seen off in the distance. Make no mistake about how quickly these storms can form, or how fast they can move.

Keep a constant eye on cloud formation, watching for these developing storms, and be certain to allow yourself plenty of time to reach a protected area, whether you're in a boat or fishing from the beach. Bear in mind also that Florida leads the nation in lightning strikes. When you see lightning nearby, don't delay; seek shelter immediately.

Last, there is a danger when wading to forget that, while the water is relatively warm, it's a long way from normal body temperature. Wading waist-deep or less generally creates no problem, but keeping the chest area submerged for any length of time can sap body heat, which creates the potential for hypothermia. If you begin to feel chilled while wading, get out and warm up a while.

Florida's ecology presents unique opportunities for fishing, but it also creates unique weather conditions. As the Midwest has a near constant threat of tornadoes, and mountain areas the threat of mud or snow slides, so Florida has its own dangers. Fortunately, being observant and using a good portion of common sense will overcome those dangers.

The geologic events of the past have combined to give us a unique ecology that presents sport fishermen opportunities not available elsewhere. Take advantage of the great fishing in the skinny water and you'll want to come back for more.

Guaranteed.

Chapter 2

What About Tackle?

Before we get into tackle selection, there's one thing we need to get out of the way, lest you be left with the wrong impression. For a dozen or so years during the '60s and '70s I was a field tester for Abu-Garcia, one of the world's largest manufacturers of fishing reels. I was fortunate enough to work not only on proposed improvements to proven reels, but also on the development of new models, such as the now-famous Cardinal series of spinning reels.

I'd like to be able to tell you this experience does not in any way color my opinion concerning fishing tackle, but the fact is it just ain't so.

Although I do own reels that are not Garcia products, I rarely use them. I'm simply stuck on the reels I know best. I can completely strip my bait-casting and spinning reels, clean them, and put them back together properly. I'm familiar with their features, what individual reels were designed to do, and how much I can safely exceed those designs.

There are, however, many brands of reels that perform quite well. Daiwa, Penn, Shakespeare, and Shimano, to name just a few, all have reels equivalent to models made by Abu-Garcia, and those reels will probably work as well, as long and as smoothly as the Garcia models I use. Consequently, if I use a Garcia model as an example of a suitable reel, please don't assume I'm implying it's the only reel that will do the job under discussion.

On the assumption that you aren't completely new to the sport of angling, I won't waste time on the differences between various types of tackle. I'll assume you know a bait-casting reel from a fly reel. Consequently, unless otherwise specified, what follows applies to both spin and conventional gear. Fly tackle will be handled separately.

Let's Get Reel

We have to start somewhere, so we might as well start with the reel. Bait-casting (conventional), open-faced spinning and fly tackle can all be used effectively inshore. While there are of course exceptions, and some models of closed-face reels are made well enough for use in saltwater, most simply don't have the line capacity or the drag system for the fish you're likely to encounter. You could safely use a closed-face reel from a pier, fishing for flounders for example, but what do you do when the occasional 10-pound redfish wanders by and decides your shrimp would make a nice snack?

Either save the closed-face reels for freshwater or accept the fact that you'll lose an inordinate number of fish you simply can't keep away from pilings, trees, or Cuba. Using light tackle (10-pound test or less) or ultra-light (under 6-pound test) for smaller fish will add greatly to your enjoyment, but the same caveat applies; you'll lose a few fish now and then.

If you're from the Midwest, or some other area lacking saltwater, you've probably fished primarily in freshwater, with perhaps a trip or two each year to do battle with some bruisers of the briny. Consequently, you probably already realize, or have been advised, that your light freshwater tackle is totally unsuited for Florida's inshore waters.

Not true.

It would probably have been true twenty-five years ago, perhaps even less far back, but it isn't true today. Twenty or more years ago, many reels intended for largemouth bass and other freshwater species, while built well enough, were simply not made of materials capable of withstanding the frighteningly corrosive nature of saltwater, nor the punishment of which saltwater fish are capable. Today's reels are far removed from the delicate machinery of yesteryear, at least for the most part. Unless your current gear is from the absolute bottom of the line (in which case it won't matter if it were originally intended for saltwater use, anyway), a rod/reel combination from a major manufacturer should be usable in Florida's coastal waters.

If in fact the gear you already own is unsuitable for use in inshore Florida, it's more likely to be due to size than to quality. Much will depend on your individual level of skill as an angler, and only you know that.

As an example, one of my favorite combinations is a 4600CB Ambassadeur, loaded with 8- or 10-pound-test line and mounted on a Berkley Series One rod, but I wouldn't recommend it unless you have a fair amount of experience fighting strong fish capable of stripping large quantities of line. The 4600 is a narrow-spool reel, and has a maximum line capacity of 150 yards of 10-pound-test line. Is a big redfish capable of running that far when hooked? You bet, and a 50-pound tarpon could run that far before he even realizes he's hooked. Figuratively speaking.

But the 4600 is a well-made little reel, with a great drag system and quality parts. It has a Fastcast Bar for one-handed casting, which is one of those things most people feel so-so about until they get used to using it. Then they wonder why they didn't get a reel with that feature years before they did. (There is a danger to the release bar drive disengagement, regardless of the brand of reel; you must take care not to accidentally press the bar while fighting a fish, or you'll be presented with a backlash more complex than any regulation ever established by Congress.)

If you have a reel equivalent to the 4600 (at this writing, the Abu-Garcia equivalent is the 4600CI), you feel the construction, drag and materials are up to the challenge, and you feel more comfortable using it than you would with another reel, go ahead and use it. A better choice would be the Ambassadeur 5500, or an appropriately sized Daiwa ProCaster, Shimano Calcutta, or similar reel.

For spinning reels, I use the Abu-Garcia Cardinal Series, mostly the 754 or 755 for general fishing with 12-pound-test line, the 654GT for under 12-pound-test and the 862GTX for two- and four-pound test line. These are relatively old reels, and the model names and numbers have changed. Equivalent reels available today would be the Cardinal Classic Model 4, the Ultracast Model 64 and the Ultracast 62, respectively. Other excellent choices would be the Daiwa SS Tournament 1600 or the Shimano Spheros 4000.

Reel Drag

Just remember the line limitations, and don't overload the drag system. When using lighter tackle, whether spin or casting, it's a good idea to fish with the drag just a bit lighter than needed, and add drag with your finger or hand on the spool. Your drag washers won't overheat, and the automatic increase in drag as a fish runs out line won't matter as much.

Possibly the most talked about and least understood element of the physics of fishing is the reel drag. Set it properly before the first cast, so you won't be tempted to change it while fighting a

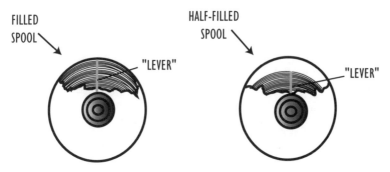

Figure 2-1. The smaller the diameter (less line) of your spool, the greater the pull required to overcome the drag, so it's advisable to set the drag as light as possible to avoid a broken line.

fish. When the drag is under a strain, it's nearly impossible to regulate with any degree of accuracy just how much change is being made, and more than one fish has broken off when someone decided to tighten the drag "just a tad," and it seized. The same can happen when trying to decrease the drag. Try to back it off just a little bit while it's under the strain of a big fish, and you end up with no drag at all. Then you try to add some back and . . . bye-bye fish.

Let's talk about that automatic drag increase a moment.

On the surface, it would seem that if a line is rated to break at 20 pounds of tensile pull, setting the drag to allow the spool to turn at anything less than 20 pounds of pull would prevent the line's breaking. Why not? With 20-pound test, and the drag set so that it starts slipping at 15 pounds of pull, you have a margin of 5 pounds.

Not so. In fact, for line of 20-pound class, the drag should be set at between 4 and 7 pounds. Use a scale to set the drag, at least until you gain experience.

(Jim McIntosh, product manager at Abu Garcia, made it a point to remind me to mention that drag settings should be measured with the reel mounted and the line run through the guides, and he's right. Do not simply attach the scale to the line coming off a reel; measure it as though you were striking or fighting a fish.)

There are many factors that must be considered in arriving at the figures for both the initial, or striking, drag, and the fighting drag.

Let's examine a couple of them.

If we start out with a drag setting of 20 pounds, it will take 20 pounds of pull to cause the drag to slip, with the reel full. But if, between the length of the cast and the distance a fish has run, the spool is reduced to half its diameter, it will take 40 pounds of pull to slip the drag. Here's why.

As the effective diameter (which will vary according to the amount of line remaining on the spool) decreases, the amount of pull required to allow the spool to slip increases. Frank Moss, in his excellent book *Modern Saltwater Fishing Tackle*, expresses this phenomenon as an equation; $X = A/B \times W$, where X is the new line tension, A is the original (filled) spool diameter, B is the new diameter (filled minus line cast out and line run off by the fish), and W is the original drag setting in pounds.

Picture a line drawn from the axle to the top edge of a full spool. This line represents a lever, against which the fish is pulling, and which ultimately acts upon the spool to turn it. At half capacity, this lever is reduced to half its length. Half the leverage means twice the pull must be exerted to achieve the same force on the spool. (See Figure 2-1.)

I quote examples from Moss, because he has been kind enough to do the math for us. With the drag set to slip at 16 pounds, 80-pound-test line will break when the effective diameter is reduced by 20%. A 12-pound-test line with drag set to slip at 6 pounds will break if the reel spool diameter is reduced to 50% of the original diameter. Note that this is not the same thing as having half the line out; we're talking about the spool diameter, not the amount of line on the spool.

Extrapolation shows the importance of setting the drag as lightly as possible. Let's say a reel holds 150 yards of 6-pound-test line, and the drag setting, with a full spool, is at 3 pounds. A cast of 20 yards is made and a fish hits almost as soon as the lure hits the water, and runs off 30 yards of line. (If you think this is unlikely, you've never fished for jack crevalle, redfish, snook, or tarpon.)

Measuring the diameters on a test reel and working the formula provided by Moss, that comes to 9 pounds of tension. On 6-pound-test line.

When doing your calculations, remember to take into account the method of rating the line you're using. Line marked "Tournament Line," or some equivalent phrase, will be X-pound "class," meaning it will not exceed the number rating. For example, 10-pound-"class" line will break at *or below* 10 pounds of tensile pull. Line rated 10-pound-"test" will not break at less than 10 pounds. In rating lines, "class" and "test" mean opposite things. To qualify for a record for a given species, for example, the line class determines the category.

It's worth noting here that Stren braided lines are rated by breaking strength at the knot, not by testing a sample piece of unknotted line.

Several other factors come into play to affect the breaking point of line, starting with the physical characteristics of the line itself. Some lines have more stretch than others, but that's both good and bad. High-stretch line can make it difficult to set a hook, but it can also absorb more of the shock of a fish's run. (It will also absorb more water, and lose strength more quickly.)

But the point is some lines stretch more than others, and can be more forgiving if the drag is a bit tight.

Note that we haven't even considered the drag of the line through the water, and any weeds it might pick up.

So what's the solution?

Well, there are two. One is to get a reel with both a striking and a fighting drag. Learn to operate it, so that you don't have to fumble with the controls while you're fighting a fish, and know at all times how many pounds of pull each is set for.

The second is to set your drag as lightly as you can possibly have it and still set the hook. Then, as you fight the fish, simply add drag as needed by palming the spool, or just placing your finger lightly on the side of it (open-faced spinning gear) or on the line or spool itself (casting gear) as it turns. With a little bit of practice, you can acquire remarkable control over the amount of resistance you introduce.

It's pretty much a pay-your-money-and-take-your-choice proposition. You can go with the newer reels that incorporate a striking drag, or educate your finger to add resistance. But whichever way you decide, remember to check that drag and be certain it isn't too tight. No amount of mechanical genius from the engineers who design today's precision reels can save you from yourself. If you're unsure, it's better to err on the side of a too-light drag, and compensate as described.

The most important feature your reel must have is a smooth, reliable drag that can put steady pressure on a strong fish. For the most part, that's the only kind of fish you'll find in inshore Florida waters. Whether you're dunking a shrimp off a bridge or stripping a streamer fly over the top of some turtle grass on a flat, there's a greater chance of hooking a strong fighting fish than not.

Flounders, smaller trout, small snappers and such won't strip line, but just about everything else can and will.

To check the smoothness of a reel's drag, back off on the adjustment until you can suspend the reel by the line, and the weight of the reel causes the drag to slip. Watch as the reel descends; a smooth descent means a smooth drag, while a reel that drops in jerky, spasmodic increments means a drag that will cause broken lines. This test will work with either conventional or spinning reels.

Fishing from a bridge or pier, you won't need a great deal of line. If you hook a large fish from a structure, the distance he runs isn't what matters; direction is. If your drag, rod stiffness, and line strength can't keep the fish away from pilings and other obstructions, he's off, and that's where fish around bridges and piers generally head when hooked.

On the flats or in the backcountry, however, you have an entirely different situation. There, you'll find open water, with only isolated obstructions, except along the shoreline. While snook will immediately head for the first mangrove root or channel marker, fish such as redfish, tarpon, and trout are usually (never say "never" or "always") quite willing to slug it out in the open. This doesn't mean fish other than snook won't take advantage of some underwater obstruction to cut your line; they will, it just isn't uppermost in their mind as it is with snook.

If you haven't any experience with large fish, you'll be amazed at how much line something like a 10- or 15-pound redfish can peel off in a hurry.

There's no point, unless you're using something like 30-pound-test line, in trying to horse such a fish in. You must let the fish run, relying on your reel's drag and the backbone in your rod to wear it out, pumping your rod to reel in line whenever possible each time he pauses.

To sum up on reels, some things required for our type of fishing are the same as for any other kind of saltwater fishing; quality, corrosion-proof materials; close tolerance at the juncture of spool and reel body; comfortable handles; and ease of drag adjustment. Fishing inshore Florida adds the additional requirements of a high quality, smooth and strong drag, and large line capacity. That you'll match your reel to the rod and to the size line and weights you'll be casting should go without saying. So I won't say it.

The Line

When selecting your line, be certain to buy a quality brand. I'm partial to Stren and Berkley (Big Game for conventional reels and Trilene for spinning), but most of the major manufacturers offer quality line. What you're interested in is breaking strength and relative line diameter. While I've emphasized throughout this book that distance isn't as important as accuracy, it stands to reason that the easier it is to get whatever distance is called for on a given cast, the more attention you can devote to hitting the mark.

As you travel south in Florida, the ability of a line to be invisible increases in importance due to the increasingly clear water. Line tends to stand out in the gin-clear waters of the Keys.

When you consider breaking strength, don't forget to take into account the abrasion resistance of a given line. Some fish, such as snook, have fine, almost sandpaper-like teeth, which will abrade line quickly. Even those without that ability will rub your line against obstructions, their bodies, and even the bottom.

For many species, notably snook, a leader of some sort is a must. Use light wire or heavy monofilament. As snook also have line cutters built into their gill covers, the leader must be long enough to keep your line away from the bottom of the gills. As a minimum, make your leader 12 inches long, and 18 inches is even better. Wire leaders can be a bit shorter than monofilament.

Most inshore anglers find 10- to 15-pound-test line adequate, so pick a reel that will hold a minimum of 150 yards of monofilament line (or the new braided lines) in that range. If you're after the larger fish, say 100-pound tarpon, you'll need at least 200 yards of line, more if possible, and you'll no doubt want to go to at least 30-pound test. I have seen 100-pound tarpon strip nearly 300 yards of 30-pound-test line off a spinning reel before the angler could get his engine cranked to follow the fish.

Florida fish don't mess around.

Rods

Rod length will depend somewhat on your degree of skill, both in casting and in fighting a fish. Generally, most rods used on the flats are about 6 feet in length. Many ultra-lights are 5 feet or shorter, and some prefer a stick longer than 6 feet. One- or two-handed casting is a matter of choice. Artificials used inshore generally run from ⅛ ounce to ½ ounce, occasionally ¾. Seldom are they heavier; ultra-light tackle naturally uses lighter lures.

Your rod should be capable of handling lures in that range, but simply handling them isn't enough. While there are occasions when long casts must be made, for the most part casting distances on the flats are short. What's more important is that you must be able to cast accurately. In that sense, flats fishing resembles fly-casting for trout on a small mountain stream. Just as it's important to drift a dry fly right past the nose of a trout holding in the lee of the current behind a rock, so is it important to place a jig or plug within inches of a mangrove root or a "hole."

If you aren't used to this sort of casting, a bit of practice is definitely in order. One good system is to use a plastic trash bucket or barrel. When you can consistently place a ¼ ounce practice plug into a trash barrel at 40 to 50 feet, you're ready. Some people prefer to use the lid of the barrel, placing it on the ground for a target. If you can't accomplish this feat, and you feel it isn't your casting ability, you need a new rod, or at least to examine your rod, reel and line for compatibility.

Having a rod with a tip sensitive enough to make the kind of casts we're speaking of is great, but it's only a starting point. Getting the lure to the fish is only half the job; once he takes it, your rod must have the backbone to turn the fish toward you, or stop him from reaching a mangrove root or other obstruction. This ability is called "lifting power," and two of the best anglers to ever wade the skinny water, Lefty Kreh and Mark Sosin, suggest in their book *Fishing The Flats* that a rod designed for bonefish should be able to lift 2 pounds of dead weight with 6 inches of line extended beyond the rod tip. For larger fish, such as tarpon in the 100-pound range, the suggestion is 5 pounds of lifting power.

Remember, too, that you may be using different types of lures. Using a swimming plug, a stiff rod is fine, but jigs and some types of topwater plugs call for a much more active tip action.

Summing up on flats rods: some things, as with reels, remain necessities for all types of fishing. Quality reel seats: guides of ceramic material or chrome-plated stainless steel; a sufficient number of guides, properly spaced; and a comfortable handle. Fishing the flats adds a need for a tip capable of casting light weights accurately and the backbone to turn a powerful fish. Rods used for Florida inshore fish should have a blank that runs clear through to the butt.

A handle long enough for two-handed casts is helpful, but not required. For baitcasting rods, the so-called "power butt," an extension below the reel seat, is an option. Personally, I'm not comfortable with the power butt rods, but it's a matter of individual experience and comfort. If I want a longer butt, I prefer to simply go to a two-handed rod. Many like the power butt, however, and if you do, use it. The extension can definitely be helpful, allowing you to brace the rod against your forearm when fighting a strong fish.

If you'll be fishing from bridges and piers, casting capability becomes a minor factor. In some places, strong currents will require as much as four ounces of lead to hold bottom, although the norm is for much less. Add a large chunk of cut bait and you could easily be talking about a half-pound of weight. Add to that the need to put immediate and relentless pressure on fish that are frequently very large, and you come to the conclusion that a stiff, strong rod is required. Your conclusion is correct.

Unless you're fishing specifically for smaller species such as mangrove or gray snapper, flounder, sheepshead, and similar species, using small hooks and relatively light line, figure on a stiff boat rod and at least 30-pound-test line. A rod used for lake trout in deep water or similar boat rod will do just fine. If you have a lake trout rod, or one you use for large freshwater catfish, there's no reason it can't be used successfully for large fish, even snook, from bridges and piers.

Assuming your fly tackle is of high quality and was made with corrosion resistant materials, you should definitely use it on the flats. While large tarpon and snook are best taken on heavy tackle, say a 10- or even a 12-weight outfit (both because of the size of the fish and the frequent need to cast bulky streamers or other wind-resistant flies in the ubiquitous breezes) there's a definite place in the skinny water for outfits as light as 6-weight.

In addition to the tasty saltwater trout (all three kinds), small jack crevalle (up to about 10 pounds), snappers, and a dozen other species, some edible, some not, will give a good account of themselves on a 6-weight outfit, without taxing it beyond its limits. Fish such as small snook and the ever present ladyfish are great sport on light rods. I've used outfits as light as 4-weight, although most of my fly fishing is done with either an 8-weight (for trout, redfish, and small- to medium-sized snook) or a 10-weight (larger snook and tarpon). My next fly rod will be either a 6- or 7-weight.

Here are some suggestions from Captain Ben Taylor, a Keys guide:

> "I agree with the lighter rod for smaller fish for the challenge and have actually fished for bonefish with a 5-weight, although I certainly don't recommend it.
>
> "I would personally have a tough time lumping snook and tarpon together as justification for a 10-weight. I justify 10-weights for bonefish and redfish simply to handle wind and occasional outsized fish. Snook habitat and power certainly demand it if for nothing else but to avoid rod breakage with tippets heavy enough to get them out of the trees."

What the good Captain is saying here is that if you use a tippet heavy enough to turn a big snook, or drag it out of the mangrove roots, a light rod may not withstand the strain. All parts of your tackle system must be matched to your target species and to each other.

Your line should be one of the weight-forward tapers. If you currently have a floating line with a bass bug taper, that will work out perfectly. If you haven't any floating, weight-forward tapers, check out the special saltwater lines available from 3M/Scientific Anglers. They're excellent lines and, as their various names (Bonefish Taper, Tarpon Taper, etc.) imply, they're specifically designed for this type of fishing.

Because most of your fishing will be in such shallow water, the natural assumption would be that there's no need for a sinking line, as there would be, for example, if you were fishing in water 20 feet deep. However, as Captain Pete Greenan points out:

> "The weight of the fly brings the fly down, that's true; but on the first strip it comes up to the top. A sinking or sink-tip line will hold the line down longer and will also keep the fly on track in a current much better than a floater. All the Homosassa guides use them for tarpon, as do the Boca Boys."

(Homosassa is on the west coast, north of Tampa and south of Crystal River; "Boca" is Boca Grande, a fishing paradise near Charlotte Harbor, on the southwest coast.)

So don't leave your sinking lines ashore.

Captain Greenan adds:

> "Probably the most useful light tackle saltwater fly rod is a 7-weight. It's important to remember that trout, ladyfish, and jacks are often found in slightly deeper water such as 6-foot deep flats, channels such as those in the ICW [Ed. note: Intracoastal Waterway], and marina basins. Here you would need a sinking tip or full sinking line. I don't want to discount the importance of getting the fly down."

What it all boils down to is just plain common sense and knowing your abilities (in terms of casting talent and the ability to fight a fish, *including knowing when to break off a fish*) and the capabilities of your tackle. If your freshwater gear is well made, and you feel comfortable using it to fight fish that could tow a largemouth bass around all day by the tail and not know the bass was there, have at it.

Just be honest in your evaluation, and be fair to yourself, your tackle, and the fish.

Among the miscellaneous gear you normally carry, be sure you include leader material, something with which to cut it (long-nosed pliers, or some other device for removing hooks such as the Dehooker), sun blocker, insect repellent, a hat, and a good pair of polarized sunglasses.

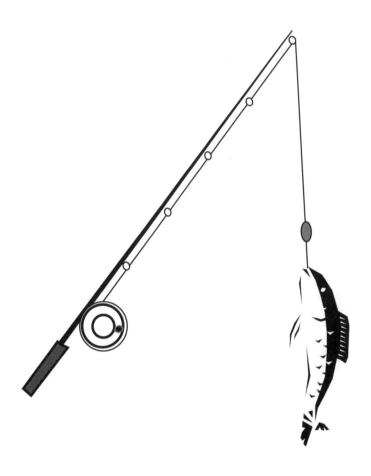

Chapter 3

Bait Wanted, Dead or Alive

The Top Two Choices for Bait

Fishing inshore in the Northeast, bloodworms, sandworms, or strips of cut squid will catch almost every species, from flounder to striped bass. In the Northwest, up Oregon way, it's ghost (sand) shrimp or herring. In Florida, the two best choices are shrimp and shrimp.

Although there are some species that don't always select shrimp from the menu, almost all will eat it if one's presented to them. Sheepshead, for example, prefer fiddler crab or pieces of clam. But put a piece of shrimp in front of one and chances are he'll eat it. They may not be the number one choice of a given species, but the odds are on your side that shrimp will be accepted.

However, the universal acceptance of shrimp as food can be a disadvantage. In fishing areas where small fish abound, such as the grass flats and mangrove edges, small but aggressive species such as pigfish and sailors' choice can become a nuisance, because they aren't excepted from this craving for shrimp.

Because they are such a ubiquitous bait, shrimp—live, dead, or frozen—are available at tackle shops throughout the state of Florida, although not all shops have the capability of keeping them alive. As a last resort, you can always go into a supermarket—and many convenience stores—and buy fresh or frozen shrimp. It's a bit more expensive, but the point is shrimp is not only a great bait, it's universally available in Florida.

Some say using shrimp for bait has the added advantage that if your luck isn't running on the good side, you can always have your bait for supper. The fact is if you do your homework and put your shrimp where the fish are most likely to be hanging out, you should be able to catch one edible species or another, as well as one or more of the dozens of catch-and-release fighters.

As with people, some fish aren't fussy about their shrimp and some are. Personally, I don't care if they're boiled, broiled, deep-fried, or steamed. I'll eat shrimp any way but raw. Snappers (just about all kinds), whiting, and most other relatively small but numerous species are on my side, here. They'll take live shrimp, dead shrimp or pieces of shrimp. Other species, while they will certainly take a dead shrimp, prefer them not only alive, but as lively as possible. In this category, you can place sea trout (especially the larger ones), snook, and tarpon.

Size takes on importance in enticing the latter three species; the larger and more lively, the better. When fishing for snook, for example, as soon as your shrimp shows signs of wear, replace it with a new one. Save the old one and use it for less fussy species. Shrimp freeze fairly well, and can be kept indefinitely if they're going to be used for bait. Some anglers soak them in a strong salt solution to toughen them before freezing; others don't bother. Usually, if only frozen and thawed once, they don't get overly mushy (Figure 3-1).

As with most generalities, there are exceptions. At age nine, our oldest boy won a summer-long fishing contest for youngsters with a 30-pound snook—caught on a small dead shrimp fished on the bottom in the St. Lucie River. So it's possible, although the odds are against it. If you want game fish, use fresh, lively shrimp, the larger the better.

Figure 3-1. This is a good-sized shrimp for snook and large trout. Note the hook in the shrimp's head. This shrimp was live-lined and moments later had taken a snook from a bridge.

Baitfish

Small baitfish such as greenback minnows, grunts, mullet, mutton minnows, pigfish, pogies (menhaden), sailors' choice, and sardines are all excellent baits. Unlike shrimp, however, they are not all found everywhere in Florida. On the Gulf Coast, especially the southwest coast, many species of small baitfish are lumped together and referred to as "white bait." Depending on the exact locale, this may include such things as mutton minnows and sardines, while in another part of the state "white bait" may mean other species.

While glass minnows, easily recognizable by what appears to be a strip of Mylar on their side, are a popular prey for many species, their delicate constitution makes it nearly impossible to keep them alive. Those caught in your cast net should be immediately released.

It isn't important which species comprise "white bait" in any given area. Basically, if they are small (5 inches or less in length), light in color and not mullet, they can be grouped together and will probably produce strikes from game fish. White bait is generally taken with a small cast net. You may not want to take the time to learn to do this if you're only visiting, but if you're a new resident and intend to use live bait often, it's a skill well worth the small investment in time and money to learn.

One word of caution, here. A number of species of fish can not be legally caught in a cast net in Florida. It's important that you know what you can and cannot legally net. Get factual information from the Marine Patrol, a tackle shop, or other reliable source before you keep any fish you net other than baitfish. Redfish, snook, and other game fish must be returned immediately and unharmed to the water. Publications abound that will help you. (See Appendix.)

There are other ways to acquire bait if throwing a cast net isn't something you care to learn. Before the commercial fishing industry developed such efficient nets, there existed in Florida a commercial hook-and-line fishery centered primarily on sea trout of various kinds, primarily spotted sea trout, and many of these fishermen caught their bait using small hooks, cane poles, and pieces of shrimp. Now that inshore netting has been virtually eliminated in Florida (by an amendment to the state constitution in 1994, effective July 1995), this type of fishing may well enjoy a resurgence in popularity.

Many recreational anglers, in fact, never stopped using this method. For pigfish, grunts, pinfish, sailors' choice, and other small fishes found on grass flats, around mangrove edges, docks, sea walls, etc., simply use a small (number 12 as a maximum, preferably smaller) hook, a bobber and a piece of bait large enough to cover the bend and point of the hook. Too large a piece of bait will be counterproductive, as it will allow the fish to nibble around the hook until the bait falls off.

Good baits include pieces of any kind of fish or shrimp or even the old freshwater standby, doughballs. Another excellent choice would be any of the "enhancers" generally used to improve the hookup ratio on jigs and other artificial lures. Cotee's "ProBait," as an example, will serve quite well in this capacity.

Baitfish spend a good deal of their time hiding, so you should fish for them around structure such as bridge and dock pilings, tree roots, and grass beds. Remember, you're fishing for extremely small fish. Trying to set the hook as you do with other species will only result in pulling the bait away from your quarry. Gently lifting the rod or pole with a tight line is all that's required.

It's a good idea to remove or file the hook's barb, as this will allow fast unhooking and get the fish into the bait well or floating bait bucket quickly and with minimum wear and tear; you probably won't even have to handle it. Do all you can to keep the baitfish fresh. A live well, aerated bait bucket or floating bait container is an absolute necessity. Simply dropping them in a bucket of water is bound to fail.

Mullet of all sizes are the next best "all around" bait in Florida. As with shrimp, mullet can be used in a variety of ways; live, whole dead mullet or cut pieces will all take fish of one kind or another. Again, for some species, the livelier the better. For redfish, sea trout, snook, tarpon, and a few other inshore predators, live finger mullet are one of the best baits. As with shrimp, the size of your quarry will dictate the size of your bait. Some fish, notably snook and tarpon, have inordinately large mouths, which means a finger mullet too large for a five-pound sea trout will be snack-sized for these bucket mouths.

Other Baits to Use

In no particular order, here are some other good baits for Florida's inshore waters. For redfish, just about any kind of "normal" crab; blue claw, calico, etc., or large pieces of shellfish such as clams. For sheepshead, fiddler crabs or clams.

The surf has one excellent bait that's unique to the shoreline; sand fleas. Shaped like a miniature tank, the sand flea burrows into the loose sand right in the wash, and can be easily caught using a sand flea rake or, frequently, just your hands. Rakes can be homemade, but aren't prohibitively expensive in most tackle shops. You may have trouble finding one inland, but most well-equipped tackle shops along the coasts carry rakes (Figure 3-2).

Using a flea rake is simplicity itself. Stand in the wash, where the water is only inches deep, and let an incoming wave pass by.

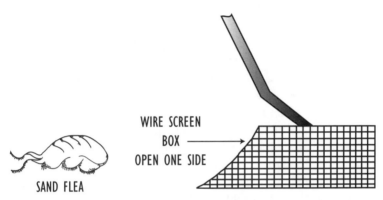

WIRE SCREEN
BOX
OPEN ONE SIDE

SAND FLEA

Figure 3-2. Sand flea rakes, home-made or store-bought, are helpful in getting some cheap, effective bait.

Just before the water starts to recede, place the rake on the sand, with the open end facing up the slope of the beach, and let the water wash through the rake. In doing so, it will carry sand, pieces of shell and sand fleas into the rake, where they are trapped by the mesh of the rake. Please return any egg-bearing females (easily distinguished by the large, orange mass of eggs on the underside of the animal) by simply placing them on the sand, where they will immediately burrow into it.

Just about anything that swims along the beach will eat sand fleas, from redfish and snook to pompano and whiting. Sand fleas are, in fact, the bait of choice for the latter two species. Generally, the larger the flea, the better bait it will be. Two or three smaller fleas can be strung together on the same hook if necessary.

Shrimp can be hooked through the tail or through the head. If you employ the latter, be careful to avoid piercing the brain, visible as a dark spot. Captain Chris Mitchell, a guide who fishes primarily in the Charlotte Harbor area, prefers hooking shrimp through the tail, for two reasons; they seem to live longer and they are easier to cast. Because the reason for hooking a shrimp through the tail or the head is to do the least damage and keep the bait lively, it follows that it doesn't much matter how or where you place the hook if using dead shrimp.

Fish sometimes prefer one end of a shrimp to the other, for reasons unknown to me, except for the obvious possibility that the hook is simply too noticeable. If you're getting hits but not hooking the fish, try changing the location of your hook and, if that doesn't help, switch to a hook of lighter wire or a smaller size.

Fiddler crabs are generally hooked through the back, by inserting the hook into the shell at the juncture of the rear most leg on one side and coming out at the same point on the other side. For some species, such as sheepshead, hooking fiddler crabs directly through the body seems quite acceptable. Many anglers remove the pinching claw to make the crab seem easier prey. If you don't want to break it off, simply hold the crab aloft by that claw, suspended over your other hand or a bucket. The crab will accommodate by detaching the claw and dropping into your hand or the bucket. Quite helpful of the little rascals, don't you think?

Fiddlers are easily gathered using no tools other than a stick and a bucket and, possibly, a small hand shovel such as gardeners use. At low tide, nearly any muddy area will have thousands of fiddlers out scavenging a meal. There are two schools of thought on approaching them. Some prefer to stalk them, sneaking up until within lunging range. Others simply charge in and gather as many as possible before they reach their burrows. That's where the stick comes in. Often, you can jam it into the mud and pierce the burrow, preventing any further descent. Then it's a simple matter to move away the mud until the crab is exposed.

Although the pincer claw looks formidable, it's incapable of doing any serious damage to all but the most tender of human hands. Putting some wet grass or seaweed and a small amount of water in the bucket should ensure lively fiddler crabs for several hours.

Larger crabs such as blue claws are hooked through one of the points (Figure 3-3). This does little damage, and the crab will swim in a lively fashion. Crabs hooked this way are an excellent

Figure 3-3. This crab successfully enticed a 100+-lb tarpon. Note the hook through the edge of the point.

choice for tarpon and redfish. Although you can catch your own crabs, most people buy them to save time. Should you elect to catch your own, some of the most productive methods can be found in Chapter 12.

When using cut bait such as mullet (pieces of whiting, by the way, are excellent bait for, of all things, whiting), try to match the size of the bait to the size of the fish you expect to catch. The head of a mullet, hooked through the eyes, is an excellent bait for snook, but would likely be too large for most trout to bother with.

For most of the larger species, a 1/O hook is a good starting point. Smaller fish, such as flounder and sheepshead may require hooks as small as a number 4, and big trout, snook, and so on can accommodate hooks as large as 4/O. For smaller fish, hooks of lighter wire will be more effective, but don't try it with larger species. A good-sized jack crevalle or snook will straighten a light wire hook quite easily.

Put your hook in the cut bait in such a way that the point is almost at the surface, or all the way through the flesh. Burying it too deeply in the flesh will make setting the hook difficult if not impossible. Generally, fish with oily flesh, such as mullet or mackerel, make the best cut bait. This is because the oil spreads out in the water, leaving a "trail" that fish will follow to your bait. It follows, then, that bait should be changed fairly often to keep that oil slick fresh.

Chumming

Speaking of oil slicks, chumming can frequently be an effective way to bring fish close enough to find your bait. Chum can be bought at many tackle shops, or made by grinding fish and meat scraps, with a bit of oatmeal or other grain mixed in. A common trick is to add water and freeze the mixture. Lowered over the side of a boat or from a bridge or pier in a mesh bag or a bucket into which many holes have been punched, the block will slowly melt and constantly feed the slick. Many anglers prefer this over the customary periodic ladling of liquefied chum. I'm one of them, where inshore species are concerned. I prefer a steady stream of enticing blood and fish particles over intermittent heavy bursts. For species that are of vegetarian bent such as mullet, crumbled soy cake (available at farm supply and feed stores) makes a very effective chum.

The purpose of a chum slick is twofold. First, we can hope it will attract the species we're after. In addition, however, it will attract many small baitfish, on which our target species probably feeds, to some degree. Think of a chum slick as the salad bar at a buffet, with your bait the prime rib at the end of the line. Fish will work their way up the slick toward its source, where they will find your entree awaiting, after having worked up a good appetite on the hors d'oeuvres.

It's not necessary to serve cocktails.

One Last Word on Using Bait

By its very nature, bait is non-selective. In other words, anything can come by and decide to eat it. This isn't common when using artificial lures. Although catfish and even sheepshead have been caught on artificial lures, it isn't generally the case. For the most part, artificial lures will target certain species; bait will not.

If what happens to eat your bait is not one of the species you're after, keep one thing in mind; it isn't the fish's fault. You put something out there to be eaten, and something else came along and ate it. If you fish Florida long enough or often enough, one of the things you will, sadly, eventually see is unwanted "trash" fish thrown on bridges or along the side of a road. It's commonly (and mistakenly) believed that saltwater catfish are inedible, and they are the most frequent victims of the incredibly stupid and short-sighted "If I can't use it, it deserves to die" attitude. If you don't want it, put it back. Not only is it the ethical thing to do, wasting fish is against Florida law.

A word of caution. Some species are armed and dangerous. Sting rays and catfish in particular can "put a serious hurtin' on you." If you aren't familiar with these fish and with the proper way to handle them, don't take any chances; cut the hook off and let them fall back into the water. The spikes on catfish and sting rays are quite capable of piercing a shoe, especially the soft shoes many of us have taken to wearing, such as sneakers, and a catfish spike in the foot will frequently lead to a trip to the emergency room. Don't try to kick a catfish back into the water. Not ever.

Chapter 4

Fishing from Bridges and Piers

The Fish Are at Your Feet

Over the fifty-plus years I've been fishing, I've watched and fished alongside many anglers from various parts of the country, and one particular type of fisherman never ceases to amaze me. This man, woman, or child marches resolutely to the farthest point on a pier and casts just as far as he or she can.

What I don't know is why.

Bridges and piers aren't such good places to fish only because they get you far out over the water. They're good places to fish because they attract fish. So why go to a place that will attract fish, then cast as far from that place as you can? Beats me. Most fish caught from structures are caught within fifty feet of that structure, and usually less. There are various reasons for this, all obvious on examination. Let's look at a few reasons fish like to hang out around structure of any kind.

First, there's the matter of food supply. The pilings or other supports that hold up a bridge or pier quickly become home for various marine organisms such as barnacles, clams and oysters, as well as marine algae, grasses, and other delicious graze. These attract several species that feed on them and an equal number that feed on the feeders. Some feed directly on what's attached to the pilings, others feed on the leavings. Pinfish, for example, haven't the dental equipment needed to crack open a barnacle, but will readily join in on the feast when a sheepshead does so. (See Figure 4-1.)

Figure 4-1. Many communities in Florida offer public fishing piers such as this one at Cedar Key on the Gulf Coast. Newly built after a major storm in 1993, it harbors flounder, redfish, and seatrout.

A trend started decades ago that really caught on in the '70s is that of leaving the ends of a bridge intact when the time comes to replace it. With only the center sections removed, the result is two fishing piers extending into or at least relatively near the main channel from each side. There are several advantages to this, including the obvious one of not having to concern yourself with vehicular traffic.

In addition, there is no wait while new pilings build up the marine growth that will attract fish, as the old pilings and supports already have flourishing colonies of animal and plant life, and fish are already accustomed to hanging around the old structure.

In a more profligate time, it was a favorite trick of some bridge and pier fishermen to use a long pole to scrape barnacles and other shellfish off pilings to create a chum line and attract various species. Not only is this recklessly wasteful behavior frowned upon today, in many places it's illegal. In any event it isn't necessary.

What's important to understand is that the reason fish hang around bridges is the marine growth that adheres to it and to its supports. So that's where to fish—near the pilings.

This isn't to say there's never a reason to cast out from a structure, that you must always drop your line straight down. There are times when it's to your advantage to cast away from a structure, for example to reach a known patch of grass or a hole, slough, or cut. What I referred to above is the tendency to automatically cast as far as possible when that may not only hold no advantage, but actually may be counter-productive. Barring a provable reason to do otherwise, keep your bait or lure close to the structure; that's most likely where the fish are. Yes, there are exceptions. This is, after all, Florida.

Tidal currents frequently run quite fast under bridges and piers, creating tough swimming for small baitfish and rendering shrimp all but helpless swimmers. This works to the advantage of predatory fish, which are relatively quite strong, and excellent swimmers. This is one reason fishing from such structures is usually best when the tide is running well, either in or out.

Structures also offer protection from overhead, and things behind which fish can hide, either to escape detection or to lie in wait for dinner to pass by.

For some species, there's one more advantage, and that comes at night.

Most bridges and some fishing piers in Florida are lighted at night, if for no other reason than they are used by vehicles. Generally, the lights run along one side of the bridge. This casts two shadows; one nearly straight down from the edge of the structure and the other, on the side opposite the lights, anywhere from 10 to 30 feet out, depending on the width of the bridge and the height of the lights.

Many species, notably snook, tarpon, and ladyfish, use the shadow for concealment, drifting with the tidal current and swimming just enough to maintain proximity to the edge of the shadow. Quite often, these fish can be seen from the bridge, if you use a little trick.

Generally, there's a space in the concrete railing of bridges, and kneeling to stick your head through this opening will greatly reduce the glare of the surrounding lights. A cap with a bill will also help, as will cupping your hands around the sides of your head. Wait a few minutes for your eyes to adjust and you should be able to see snook in the shadow. Often, a snook will swim in open view, apparently not caring if he's seen or not. These fish are not generally feeding actively, and have led to the frustration of many anglers over the years.

The ones you're looking for are lurking in the shadows like a mugger in a darkened doorway. Frequently, they will stay under the bridge, sometimes they'll move out from it a couple of yards, but the active feeders seldom venture out into the light. Live-lining a large shrimp or a lively baitfish will generally coax a snook into hitting. (See Chapter 8 for details.)

Although snook are a prime target for night anglers on bridges, there are other species that can also be a great deal of fun. Ladyfish will generally hang off from the structure a bit, usually 20 to 50 feet. While they readily take bait, I recommend using an artificial so as to reduce the possibility of damage, as you'll want to release them. Ladyfish will jump right on a MirrOlure or similar swimming plug and topwater lures such as the Zara Spook. Be sure to flatten the hook barbs for easier release.

Two other residents seen at night are the lookdown and the moonfish. Both are silvery white and saucer-shaped with sharply sloping heads. Quite small, they will give a good account of themselves on tackle sufficiently light. They'll take small shrimp and very small baitfish, and frequently will attack a small piece of white cloth impaled on a hook. Use hooks in panfish size, number six or smaller. Both are edible.

In the southern part of the state, pompano can frequently be taken in the summer (the farther north, the shorter the time frame) from bridges, using shrimp, small crabs, or jigs. Preferred color for jigs is all yellow, with yellow and white a close second. In some places, anglers don't even bother with a rod and reel, preferring to jig with a cane pole where the bridge or pier is close enough to the water. (Some old-timers still use a cane pole for snook, securing a long length of stainless steel leader wire directly to the pole. When a fish is hooked, they hold it at the surface and lower a bridge gaff or net. It's effective at times, but hardly sporting.)

While trout will be found directly under a bridge in many cases, most often they will be in the grass beds which frequently lie a few yards away from the bridge, if the water is sufficiently shallow to support grass.

Using the proper bait, it's possible to catch nearly all inshore species from bridges and piers in Florida. Bridges near inlets and passes will be visited by cobia and mackerel in season, and a few will even yield king mackerel and bonito, especially in the Panhandle.

Snappers of various varieties can be caught using shrimp, as can Atlantic croakers (north of Cape Canaveral on the east coast, Tampa on the west), grunts, some types of groupers and several members of the drum family.

Sheepshead can be found near the pilings, along with a few kinds of sea bass in certain areas, and jetties are a favorite among those seeking this tasty and crafty fish.

They're regular fish cornucopias, those Florida bridges.

You'll want a stiff rod and heavy line, as suggested in Chapter 2. One of the established facts of fishing in the waters of inshore Florida is that the number of species you can encounter is incredible, and nowhere is that more evident than around bridges, jetties, and piers. You may be fishing for small snappers or for lookdowns when a 20- or 30-pound snook takes your bait. As a result, you should always assume you'll have to deter a large fish whose mind is bent on reaching a piling around which he can take a few turns of your line.

Live-Lining

An extremely effective way to fish from bridges is a method known as "live-lining," and practiced not only from bridges and piers, but from boats. Live-lining involves the use of live bait, generally shrimp or crabs, but also small baitfish. Hook the bait in the appropriate place, using the smallest, lightest hook that will be sufficiently strong, and allow the bait to drift with the current passing under the bridge. Most live-line anglers keep the bait close to the bridge, lifting it for another drift once it gets under the bridge, much like a cane pole fisherman placing a worm next to a brush pile.

Chris Krueger, of Matlacha (pronounced mat-la-SHAY), a small town on the way to Captiva Island, is one of the most successful live-liners for snook I've ever come across. Chris generally uses a short-shanked No. 1 or 1/0 hook, and prefers a bronzed Mustad. She joins line to leader with a blood knot, unless she feels the need for a little bit of weight, in which case she uses a swivel to join them. Depending on the time of year and availability, Chris uses either small ladyfish or hand-picked shrimp for bait. (See Figure 4-2.)

She flips her bait into the light beyond the bridge shadow on the upcurrent side, allowing it to drift into the shadow and under the bridge. When fishing the downcurrent side, she swings the bait under the bridge and lets it drift out. She prefers the upcurrent side, and generally has seen and targets a particular fish or group of fish.

Working the Structure

As stated earlier, the advantage of fishing bridges and jetties lies in more than just getting you farther out on the water. They attract fish. If you're using artificial lures, the best way to cover the greatest amount of productive water is to cast parallel to the bridge or jetty, provided you can do so without interfering with other anglers. You may even be better off not going onto the structure in the first place, but wading in a few feet alongside it or

Figure 4-2. Live-lining a shrimp at night from the bridge over Matlacha Pass got Chris Krueger this nice snook.

fishing from an apron. Wading alongside is a very productive way to fish a jetty, especially right at daybreak, when the fish have not yet left for deeper waters. (See Figure 4-3.)

It isn't always possible to do, but where legal and safe, wading and casting parallel to a bridge, sea wall or jetty allows you to cover productive areas while making it more difficult for fish to see you. Depending on the time of day and the water and weather conditions, you can use live bait, jigs, and both topwater and swimming plugs. If the structure casts a shadow from lights at night, try to work the line of the shadow. This is an excellent method for snook and large trout.

When fishing a bridge or pier, cast upcurrent and allow the lure to swing in toward the bridge as you retrieve it, thus describing an arc. You can also use this method with live shrimp. At a jetty, stay close to the rocks and cast parallel to it for snook and redfish. For sheepshead, snappers, and other small fish found around jetties, it's best to stay on the jetty, trying several places until you begin to get hits. These fish don't roam as much as redfish and snook,

Figure 4-3. The 1,600-ft pier at Panama City is the longest on the Gulf of Mexico, and allows winter anglers to catch species normally found offshore, such as kingfish.

preferring to find a good spot to hide and feed, and staying there for quite some time.

You may need a few pieces of specialized gear to make the most of bridge fishing. If you want to use live bait, you'll need a bait container with a line long enough to reach the water so you can lower it and keep your bait as fresh as possible. Two cautions: one, be sure your line is not so long as to interfere with others; and two, check it frequently for debris. Floating seaweed, marine grasses, and other objects can build up enough to put a serious strain on the line or the bucket's handle and should be cleared as soon as you notice any.

If you plan to fish for larger fish, you'll need some sort of specialized landing gear. A long-handled gaff may work well from a jetty or low pier, but a bridge gaff or bridge net will probably be required in most cases. The bridge gaff is simply a small grappling hook on a long line. Most are homemade, and include a wooden handle in which the hook is stored.

A bridge net is a wide-mouthed mesh net on a circular frame, which is attached by several smaller lines to a single heavy line.

When using a bridge net, do not try to scoop the fish with the net. Instead, lower the net beneath the surface, guide the fish over it, then lift the net. An accomplice makes the procedure much simpler, and you'll find no shortage of help if you need it.

Here's another advantage of fishing close to a bridge, or more to the point, a good reason for not trying to cast too far. Alongside many bridges you will find telephone and other cables as well as power lines, running between poles that parallel the bridge. Many sea birds can be seen hanging from those lines, hooked while trying to get a piece of bait off a hook dangling from a length of fishing line that wrapped around the cable or wires when someone tried to put a little extra into a long cast and got the cast a little too high. Whether you like or dislike pelicans, sea gulls and terns, I think you'll agree dying of starvation or thirst while hanging from a cable is not the kind of death any living creature should have to endure.

Spillways

There's one final type of structure that needs to be explored, and that is the spillway. While most spillways are found in the southern, flat sections of Florida, there are some throughout the state. Spillways are dam-like structures, sometimes movable and sometimes fixed, over which excess water is allowed to drain from canals. (See Figure 4-4.)

Because nearly all Florida's freshwater comes from rain, it behooves agricultural interests to dam some of it and pump water out of drainage canals as needed. In addition, drainage canals provide an outlet for water from thunderstorms and other sources of intense rainfall, such as gales and hurricanes. Fixed spillways simply hold water behind them until it exceeds their height and spills over. The movable ones can be adjusted to open, usually from the bottom, when a predetermined level is reached.

When water rushes over or through a spillway, freshwater panfish, shrimp, and other edible goodies are swept with it. This is especially true of the movable type, because the water comes out in a rush when the spillway is opened. The force of the water

Figure 4-4. The water thundering through an open spillway in south Florida is a virtual dinner bell for many species and almost guarantees you'll catch snook.

coming through this latter type of spillway is tremendous, and even strong swimmers are advised to wear a flotation vest when fishing near one.

The general method is to stand on one of the spillway aprons or the shoreline on the downstream side of the spillway, toss a swimming plug or jig up into the turbulent water, and let it work back toward you, keeping a tight line at all times. Don't think the turbulence is too great for fish. It is for the fish being swept over or through the structure, but snook and tarpon, especially, can swim against—and feed in—amazingly swift water, and are frequently taken right at the base of the spillway in water that would appear impossibly turbulent.

When a movable spillway opens up, the thunder of water emanating it is like the ringing of a dinner bell to any fish nearby, and nearby might be a mile away. Jacks, snook, and tarpon are especially fond of feeding at this moving smorgasbord, rushing in and scooping up smaller fish and shrimp rendered completely helpless by the force of the current and the low visibility of the silt-laden water.

Generally, it takes a few hours after a major rainfall for the water to get too high for containment, depending on how high the water was initially. Experienced spillway fishermen generally keep a close watch on the water level during the rainy season and can predict within a few hours when the gates will open. The feeding frenzy generally starts within an hour or two after the opening.

There are few guarantees in fishing, but taking snook and tarpon at a spillway that's running strong is about the easiest way there is. Even when the daily bag limit for snook was 4 over 18 inches, it rarely took more than an hour to get that limit, and that was back in the '70s and late '60s, when snook were nowhere near as numerous as they are today.

One last point. As pointed out in Chapter 10, in most cases no saltwater fishing license is needed when fishing from a structure permanently attached to land, but there are exceptions. Don't take any chances. Check with the Florida Marine Patrol if unsure, or ask where you buy bait or tackle. More often than not, people working at a tackle shop will know exactly which local bridges or piers require a license.

There are many ways and places to catch fish in Florida without using a boat. Fish those bridges, jetties, and piers properly and you'll be in position to take advantage of a wide variety of species that are great fighters and excellent table fare.

Chapter 5

Fishing the Flats

There are literally thousands of miles of skinny water in Florida, which is good. Nearly all of it looks as though it would be productive, which is bad. The trick is to learn what makes one area productive, and another apparently infertile, or perhaps just less fruitful. One of the best, most productive types of "terrain" is what is known as "the flats." But you need to know what it is that sets one grass or mud flat apart from others, or what's different about one section of a particular flat.

Scouting the Flats

You won't always find fish on a flat, simply because they aren't always there. For the most part, if game fish are going to feed on a flat, they move onto it with the rising tide, feed through the flood, then move back off the flat as the tide drops. (There are exceptions, such as redfish, but you knew there would be.) Obviously, then, it's wise to be aware of the exact time(s) of the tide(s) on a given day. (Figure 5-1.)

Ideally, high tide would be shortly after daylight or just before dark. This puts the fish in an area where you can find them at just the time they are most likely to be feeding.

Figure 5-1. Completely covered at high tide, these holes and channels will be invisible from a distance, but will attract and hold such species as redfish, seatrout, and in south Florida, snook.

Like the fish, you can move onto the flats with the rising tide, do your thing and be gone before the day's heat arrives or it gets dark. This is not to say you have to leave at dark; most fish that feed on the flats do so throughout the night, if the tide is right. Unfortunately, so do the mosquitoes and other biting insects, so if you fish at night, take along plenty of repellent.

It's a good idea to make scouting trips to flats on a low tide, during the day. This allows you to locate many of the cuts and channels hidden at high tide. These channels are the highways of the skinny water. Fish move back and forth between different areas and move across flats using these highways. Knowing precisely where they are gives you a distinct advantage. Find the main channels and you know where fish are most likely to enter and leave the flats. This doesn't mean that's the only way fish will go on or off a flat. It's just a starting point. But, because you have to start somewhere, why not a place with an extra reason for holding fish?

Don't think in human terms. Human engineers would carve a straight line from the deep channel of, say the Intracoastal Waterway (ICW), directly to the nearest flat, then lay out a neat grid of cuts on the flat itself. Nature doesn't work that way. The channels may be anywhere, from the drop into the ICW, to right along the edge of the mangrove trees, to anywhere between the two. They may run perpendicular or parallel to the shoreline. That's why it's a good idea to scout a new area at low tide, when these channels are more likely to be visible. A bright, high sun also helps, as it emphasizes the difference in water depth, so if temperature and your available time allow, try for mid-day scouting. Polarized sun glasses are a definite advantage.

Don't look for major differences. You're not searching for the Marianas Trench. The difference between the water depth in a channel or cut used by fish moving around in an area and the surrounding water may be as little as a foot, and possibly even less, although you will find some channels three and four feet deep. At dead low tide, there may be only inches of water on a particular flat, or even no water at all. If so, those channels will stand out like a peacock at a swine show. So will the holes, which, like the channels, may have only a foot or so more water than the surrounding area. (See Figure 5-2.)

Figure 5-2. This oyster bar will bring redfish looking for small baitfish and crabs and other marine life, but if you haven't scouted it at low tide, you'll never know about that hole.

But there are some deep holes on the flats, too. For example, there's a hole off Cedar Key, north of Crystal River on the west coast, that's about fifteen or twenty feet deep. At low tide, you can't even push a boat to it, much less pole or run there by motor. But when the tide drops, many of the trout on that flat congregate in this deep hole and wait for the tide to turn. I know a group of anglers who went in there on the dropping tide, while there was still enough water, and fished all through the low tide in that little hole. They caught trout on nearly every cast. (The group was fishing a fun catch-and-release tournament and quantity was important. They knew they'd be there for the whole morning, until the incoming tide put enough water on the flat to float their boat, but they figured the wait would be worth it to catch a lot of fish.)

Working the Flat

Okay, you've scouted a particularly promising grass flat. The grass looks good; dark green color, high growth, and you've seen many wading birds working the area, usually an indication there's a good population of small baitfish and crustaceans in town. You run to it, getting there just as the sun peeks over the eastern horizon. High tide is about two hours off. Now what?

First, don't run directly to the edge of the area you're going to fish. Stop your boat a few hundred yards off and go the remainder by drifting, poling, or using your electric motor. Stealth is the key. Roaring at full throttle up to an area you plan to fish is one of the surest guarantees of failure.

While we're on the subject, it's a good idea to give another angler working a flat plenty of room. There are few things more frustrating than working hard to locate fish, only to have them run off by some inconsiderate boater who roars through the area. Remember, sound travels better in water than it does in air. You can imagine what a Super Monster Turbo 150 sounds like to a fish. Be courteous, and give others plenty of room. The Golden Rule applies.

It's quite possible for more than one angler to work the same flat at the same time, provided they both know what they're doing. Generally, however, it isn't what would be called a great idea. If someone's using the flat you had intended to try, it's better to simply try another; it isn't as if they are scarce. If you must fish a flat already being worked by someone, at the very least don't get ahead of him. Wait to see which direction he's moving, then get as far behind him as you can.

Yes, you'll be working water he's already fished, but if he knows the proper way to fish a flat, the fish won't have been spooked too badly. If he doesn't, it won't matter if he's already fished the same water or not; he's probably run the fish off, anyway. Remember, too, that new fish may have arrived after he did, in the area he's already fished.

An exception to this rule is the case of two anglers who know each other and want to fish an area together, using two boats. In this case, the best way would be for them to move along the flat in parallel, one near the shore and the other out along the outside edge. This gives twice the chance of locating the fish, as you'll be covering more water. When one finds the fish, the other can pole or use a trolling motor to get within casting distance. Need I point out that the way to join forces is not to crank up the main engine? I didn't think so.

We have to start somewhere, so let's assume you'll be using artificials, and describe your course of action, indicating what you'll do differently when using live or cut bait, where applicable.

Run as close to the area you'll be fishing as you can easily pole or run your electric motor, then ease your way onto the flat. You must constantly scan the water for fish or signs of them. That's one reason poling platforms on flats boats are so high; greater visibility. Some flats fishermen use two transom-mount electric trolling motors with switches mounted right on the poling platform. The switches are simple on/off devices that can be operated by foot.

With the motors locked in the straight ahead position, the boat can be maneuvered by alternating motor use. Run the starboard motor, the boat moves to port, and vice versa. Run them both at the same time (and, of course, the same speed) and the boat runs straight. Doing it this way puts the angler high above the water, for best visibility, as opposed to sitting on the bow operating an electric motor.

An alternative I've used successfully with a single, bow-mounted trolling motor is to fit a piece of garden hose or other flexible—not limp—material over the handle of the motor. Make it long enough to reach to the poling platform, and you can control both speed and direction while standing on the platform.

The two drawbacks to this system are limited range in steering, especially until you get the hang of it, and the question of what to do with the hose when it's not in use. Neither is an unresolvable problem, and the system is worth a try if you frequently fish alone. With more than one angler in the boat, obviously, one person can run the trolling motor under the direction of someone else on the poling platform.

A few words on trolling motors may save you some frustration. On the flats, there are two things with which you must contend; current and an almost ubiquitous breeze. A trolling motor that works quite well for freshwater fishing may be totally unsuitable for the flats. For most boats, 40 pounds of thrust or more will be required to maneuver with any degree of effectiveness. In addition, saltwater is highly corrosive, and your motor should be built to take that into account.

My personal choice—and this in no way implies there aren't other good choices—is the Great White model from MotorGuide, with 50 or more pounds thrust. This is definitely not one of the places in which you'll want to scrimp on your gear. The proper choice of trolling motor will pay off in a more enjoyable and more productive day. Use the Great White as a standard, and make your own comparisons. If you can find one that gives the same corrosion resistance, thrust and reliability at a price attractive to you, and you have confidence in the brand, buy it.

Whether poling, using your trolling motor or simply drifting with wind and current, you must pay close attention to the water ahead and to the side of your boat. You're looking for fish, of course, but also for signs of fish. Depending on the clarity and depth of the water, you may not be able to see the actual fish, but you can see the results of feeding or travel. Look for puffs of mud, which indicate the bottom is being stirred up. Several things cause this, including a startled fish sprinting for safety when he finally realized you were there.

Muddy water doesn't always mean you've spooked a fish, however.

Some fish, such as redfish, root around in the bottom, looking for crabs, worms, etc., and this will muddy the water. Rays and manatees will also cause this, and, even though most anglers have no desire to catch a ray, their presence may be a positive factor. If you see a ray stirring up the bottom, look carefully all around the fish. Frequently other fish will follow a ray, looking for food that escapes it, much as cattle egrets and other birds mingle with herds of grazing animals to get the grasshoppers and other insects scared up by the grazers. Manatees are also frequently followed by cobia and redfish.

Even if you don't actually see a game fish, casting near a ray stirring up the bottom is often a good idea. Among other species, cobia are widely known to seek out a ray in the hope of finding an easy meal, and a cobia in shallow water is a fight worth remembering. Just be careful when you cast around a manatee or a ray. The last thing you want to do is to foul-hook it.

Don't just look for a fish shape. Frequently, by the time you see the actual fish, you're too close and will likely spook it. This will change with experience. The distance at which professional guides and others with years of experience stalking fish on the flats can detect fish is nothing short of amazing. It is, however, a skill that can be learned. For now, look for flashes of silver or bronze, indications of moving redfish, snook, or trout ahead of the boat. Look also for small baitfish scattering wildly. This is frequently an indication of feeding game fish. You'll probably be fooled a few times in the beginning, mistaking mullet for game fish, but time will take care of that.

Don't think if you can't see fish or signs of them that all is lost. This type of flats stalking is known as "sight casting," because you first sight a fish, then cast to it. It's the most exciting way to fish the flats, but by no means the only way. So, what do you do if you can't find signs of fish, actively feeding or not?

I thought you'd never ask.

Stalking Fish

Whether in the crystal clear waters of the Keys or the more murky shallows of northern Florida, there will be discernible differences in shading, caused by variations in depth and in the nature of the bottom. Notice those lighter sections, usually circular or oval in area, looking like worn places in front of the dressers in a cheap motel. These are bare spots in the grass, frequently a tad deeper than the surrounding regions. Whether deeper or not, these bare spots are referred to as "holes," and are your target areas. (See Figure 5-3.)

Approach the holes with extreme caution. Remember how shallow the water is where you are. You're highly visible to the fish when you get fairly close. The shallower the water, the farther out you can be seen. If you're poling, do so slowly and carefully. Don't drag the pole along the bottom if you can possibly avoid it, and take extra care not to scrape or bang it against the

Figure 5-3. The light, circular shapes are "holes" where grass doesn't grow. They are favorite feeding spots for many species that lie in ambush in the surrounding grass, waiting for prey that wanders into the open.

side of the boat. Do so at the risk of spooking every fish off the flat and into deeper water. This is a good time to add a caution against noises such as tackle boxes sliding along the boat's deck. Don't make them. Even if your boat's floor is carpeted, avoid scraping boxes on the deck.

Talking is fine, but scraping anything along the deck, dropping something in the boat, banging a rod or a push pole against the side and so on will generate noises that will spook a fish every time, and startling a fish in shallow water is as irrevocable as a haircut. Spook fish more than once and you might as well move elsewhere.

Most fish spend their juvenile year(s) in these grass flats. Those that didn't form the habit of checking the air once in a while became osprey or pelican food. If they've lived long enough and gotten big enough for you to stalk them, they're suspicious of things outside the water as well as in it. Some say they recognize a boat for what it is, and the angler for what he is. I don't really know; it's been so long since I was a fish, I don't remember.

What I do know is fish in shallow water are as nervous as a wealthy bachelor in a roomful of mothers with unmarried daughters. While stalking fish on a flat, there's no such thing as "too careful."

Sometimes it isn't the fish you're after that spook, but others, unseen and unsuspected. No matter; when one goes, they generally all go, and your best move is to find another flat to fish. There's no point in chasing after the fish you've spooked. Even if you were able to come up on them again, chances are they've stopped feeding. Usually, redfish spooked off a flat will head for the edge, into deeper water. Snook will do likewise, or head back into the mangroves if the water's deep enough. Trout will generally just find another place in the grass, but trout have never been known for an excess of smarts. If you're after trout, you can generally stay where you are and fish for them after giving them a few minutes to calm down.

Assuming you don't spook any fish, stop poling as soon as you're within casting range of your target hole. Ideally, you've approached from upwind or on the upcurrent side. That way, as you cast, you'll be drifting toward the hole. Come up on the downwind or downcurrent side and after every cast you'll have to move yourself back into position. This is one of the few times when fishing inshore that distance in casting is nearly as important as accuracy. The farther you can cast and still reach your target, the less chance you'll spook the fish before you can present your bait or lure.

On the other hand, if you plan to work from one end of a flat to the other, you'll want to do so against the flow. Heading into the wind or current will give you greater steering control. It's also easier to stop the boat quickly if you see fish, to avoid running right up on them. If you see fish or fish signs, shut down the trolling motor or stop poling, evaluate the situation, and lay out a course and speed that will get you within casting distance with the least chance of alarming the fish.

Fishing the Holes in a Flat

Flounder are very likely to be right in the sand of the hole itself. That's how they feed, covering themselves with a thin layer of bottom material and changing color to blend in. (That's why flounders have both eyes on the same side of their head; for flounders, things are always looking up.) Flounders are the exception, however; most fish holding near a hole will be in the grass on the edges, not right in the hole itself. They lie there waiting for some unsuspecting or careless meal to venture out too far from the protection of the grass. Your objective is to present them with that careless meal.

Cast into the far edge of the grass if using an artificial, and work it slowly out across the open area and into the grass on the side nearest you. Don't stop working the lure if you haven't gotten a hit by the time you reach the other side of the hole. Fish will frequently follow a lure, not sure if it's edible. Many a hit has been right at the boat, just as the lure was being lifted out. Few things are more startling, as you'll discover.

A word, here, on terminology. When a fish grabs a lure, it's generally called a "hit." If he follows the lure but does not hit, it's called, imaginatively enough, a "follow." If the only sign of a predator is a break or eddy on the surface of the water somewhere in the vicinity of your lure, it's called a "swirl." Neither follows nor swirls are edible, unfortunately, but on the positive side, they don't count toward your bag limit. They do count for something, however, as we'll see in a moment.

If using bait, cast into the hole, not the grass. Drop your live bait in the grass and it will immediately hide. Being able to hide is what allowed it to live as long as it has. Dead bait can't actively hide, of course, but it sure can sink into the grass.

This is a good place for what is known as a popping cork. Essentially a cone-shaped float with a concave top, the popping cork is designed to hold the bait off the bottom at a certain depth, and also to make noises that attract fish. Your line feeds into or through (there are different styles) the cork, usually held in place by a stick in the hollow center of the cork. To adjust the depth at which your bait is hanging, you loosen the stick, pull the line so the bait is deeper or shallower, then wedge the stick back in to tighten it against the line.

With larger baits, casting is a bit tricky, as the bait and cork together make an unwieldy combination. With some practice, however, you should be able to lob it into position fairly accurately and regularly.

Having cast your bait where it will do the most good, jerk on the line periodically, to pull the cork sharply toward you. This causes a small splash and a popping sound, which is what attracts the fish you're after, and is the origin of the device's name. A popping cork makes a popping sound. Clever?

A company named Alameda Fishing Tackle Co. has come up with an innovative plastic popping float in easy-to-see red and green with a top specially designed for noise and splash. It's streamlined, so it casts more easily, and has a design that incorporates a "fast snap" easy-on and easy-off feature, and is available in five sizes. All five come either weighted or not weighted, and with or without a rattle. The rattle is a nice touch, adding a little more attraction, and is worth trying.

There are several basic ways to fish the flats with bait. First, you can simply camp somewhere, cast out your bait, and hope for the best. That's for people who haven't read this book. Having read it, you know there are more and less productive areas on any given flat, so you're certainly not going to simply leave your day in the hands of fickle fate and blind luck.

You'll look for the holes and the channels you've previously scouted and lay your baits where they'll do the most good. If you have trouble finding those channels and cuts, a second scouting trip may be necessary, and you might want to make a map this time. It needn't be anything elaborate or with great detail. You're simply making a memory-jogger that will put you on a channel even if the water's murky and it's high tide. Line up at least three shore landmarks, or stakes, navigation buoys, solitary trees, etc. Anything that won't be in a different place next time.

Put your bait, live or cut, into the hole, as described earlier. Working the channels, set yourself up a fair distance off the flat. If you know of a good cut where the difference in water depth is really marked, that would be a logical choice for a place to swim a shrimp or small baitfish. Think about what you've learned about the habits of predators on the flats, and the problem will solve itself.

For example, on a dropping tide, redfish will generally school up near the edge of the flat in the area of a good channel, feeding on fish, crabs, etc. that are having to vacate the flat, too. Place your bait in such a manner as to appear to be one of them. Fish holding off a flat in a channel tend to school up. Find one, you've usually found a school.

On the incoming tide, however, the fish will move onto the flat and spread out. You'll want to put your bait where a fish moving onto the flat is likely to check for food. Too, you must consider the type of fish you expect to find in this particular spot, and its feeding habits. Redfish will immediately spread across the flat, nose to the ground like a beagle after a rabbit, looking for crabs and other bottom dwellers.

Trout will head for the grass, seeking small fish to be sure, but mostly after shrimp. Popping corks work especially well on redfish, trout, and snook, because in each case these fish are actively cruising, looking for dinner. The noise of the cork gets their attention by seeming to be the sound of a fish feeding. They come over to see what's on the menu, and it turns out to have a hook in it. Score one for you.

These, then, are the basics of fishing on the flats. There's one more method that I've deliberately saved for last. I haven't done so out of any innate tendency to withhold the best for last, although that's the way it's worked out, but because I wanted you to first get a grasp on how and why fish feed on the flats.

Wade Fishing

This method is to use your boat strictly as transportation; a means of getting to where you believe the fish will be, and will be feeding. Once there, anchor your boat, get out, and wade the flat. You'll probably want to wait until you've fished a flat a few times before you try this, as the more intimately you know an area the better your chances of locating fish while wading.

Wading gives you several advantages, not the least of which is being less visible to the fish. The higher you are (as when you're on a poling platform) the better you can see, to be sure, but height also makes you more visible to the fish. Wading puts up to half your body (it's uncomfortable to wade and fish in water deeper than the bottom of your rib cage, although with experience it can be quite a productive way to fish) under the water, where, in all but the clearest water, it's invisible to the fish.

A second advantage comes with not being subject to movement by wind or current. When you find a particularly good looking cut or hole you can stay right where you want to be and work it over thoroughly. No maneuvering to keep the boat in position, no worries about the relative strength of wind and current. You get where you want to be and stay there until you score or you're convinced the fish aren't there. Finally, wading allows you to pick the angle at which you'll fish. Here's an example.

Let's say we have a flat with only six inches or so of water on it. Perhaps the tide's dropping, perhaps that's all this particular flat has, perhaps it usually has more but a full moon has lowered the tide more than usual. To fish the edge of the flat, where it drops off into deeper water, you may have to do it from some distance away, if your boat draws more than a few inches of water (as most do, except flats boats especially designed for skinny water fishing).

This means you'll have to keep your boat moving exactly parallel to the edge of the flat, so you're working the most productive water right where the flat drops off. Wading changes the picture entirely, because you can walk the edge of the flat, casting in such a way that you retrieve your lure parallel to the edge, meaning it's in productive water all the time.

Wading also allows you to get to inside areas that are unreachable by boat, such as shallow bays cut off by a sand or oyster bar at their opening. It does no good to find a bay with two feet of water, beautiful grass, plentiful bait to attract predators and everything else you're looking for if you can't get into the bay, and there are many such bays and lagoons in Florida. If you know how to fish while wading, you'll simply park your boat on the sand bar and walk in to the fishing area.

You'll be looking for the same things—the holes, cuts, and channels—you would if you were fishing from your boat, but now you won't have the height advantage offered by the poling platform. This is why you'll want to wait until you're very familiar with a particular flat before wading it. You can easily walk within fifty feet of a hole and not see it, while wading.

That's one disadvantage. Another is that you can carry only a limited number of baits with you, as there's no place for a tackle box. You'll be limited to what you can carry in a couple of pocket-sized plastic boxes, for the most part. You might find a "fanny pack" particularly helpful. You'll also have to carry a net or gaff with you, and something on which you can string your fish.

Disadvantage three is the novelty of casting, working a lure, and fighting a fish while standing in waist-deep water. This is the least significant and most easily overcome drawback to wading, as it only takes time and experience. It will definitely be awkward at first, but you'll get used to it very quickly.

The fourth disadvantage is that there is some danger inherent in walking around dragging injured (read "easy prey") fish on a stringer behind you. I have never known anyone to get bitten while doing this, but I have known several people who had rays, sharks, and other fish decide the stringer represented a buffet table, and try to help themselves to the catch. Not a major problem, but one of which you should be aware.

Finally, there are three dangers in wading. First, you need to be sure you don't step in a hole or in mud or muck that will trap your foot, or in which you'll sink up to your knees. Stepping in a hole while wading is about like thinking you were on the last rung of a ladder and stepping off, while you were actually on the second rung. You won't break anything, but the jar will definitely get your attention.

The second danger is more serious, and it involves sting rays. Rays are easily seen when cruising across the flats, with their wide bodies and their "wings" flapping away. They also, however, have a nasty habit of lying motionless on the bottom, waiting for dinner. In all but the clearest of water, and sometimes even then, it's possible to step right on a ray.

Rays don't care for this. They have a very poorly developed sense of humor, and definitely do not consider this a fun way to pass the time. To make their point (pun intended), they will retaliate by stabbing you in the foot or leg with the barb on their tail. This is very painful. To the stickee, not the sticker. The stickee being, of course, the wader who stepped in already-occupied space.

How painful is it? Well, pain, of course, is subjective. What's excruciating to one person may be only a major nuisance to another. I fished eight or nine hours after being stuck by a ray, but it hurt like the devil all the time. A more sensible person would have quit for the day and gone to an emergency room for treatment or at least an examination and a tetanus booster, and that's what my recommendation is. If you do get stuck by a ray, stop fishing, clean the wound, and seek medical treatment immediately.

The fact that I'm stubborn is no incentive for you to be in pain any longer than you have to. I mention my having continued fishing only so you understand that being stuck by a sting ray, while painful, is something you'll get over. It just won't seem so at the time, and there is always the possibility of an allergic reaction or an infection.

The best way to avoid getting stuck is to learn to shuffle your feet as you wade. Instead of taking a normal step, slide your foot across the bottom. The theory is that this will allow your foot to contact, but not trap, the ray, which will immediately take off for safer environs. It probably works. I have bumped into many rays with my feet while sliding them in the approved manner, and each time the ray has scooted off with no injury to either of us.

Lest you be unduly alarmed, let me point out that in thirty years of wading Florida and Caribbean waters, I have been stuck exactly one time. On that occasion, I was with Captain Pete Greenan in Turtle Bay, an area of Charlotte Harbor down near Boca Grande on the west coast.

I had an assignment for a story that required some specialized photos—redfish taken on a fly—and knew from past experience Captain Pete could deliver, so we went to some flats he knew and, sure enough, got the pictures. On the way back to the boat, we entered a small area of very soft bottom, and rather than skirting the muddy section as Greenan did, I elected to go through it, as it was not as deep as where he waded, and I was carrying not a rod, but a camera. I opted for shallower water and tougher walking, rather than risk getting my camera wet.

Because the bottom was so soft, it was impossible to slide my feet; I had to lift them. After one step, I came down on a ray, pinning it to the bottom, and was immediately made aware of its displeasure by a sharp, painful blow to my instep, accompanied by a burning sensation. When we got back to the boat and I removed my wading shoe, the puncture was obvious.

So the point is it can happen. It doesn't happen often, if you're careful. My encounter came recently, after 30 years of uneventful wading in tropical and subtropical waters, and then under circumstances I could have, but didn't, avoid. Nature is unforgiving of carelessness, and one can hardly fault the ray for defending itself against a perceived threat. Another point is that the shoes I use for wading are simply low-cut canvas shoes, and there are special wading shoes available which would have afforded more protection.

If you feel the possibility of being stuck by a ray is sufficient reason to avoid wading the flats, you'll get no argument from me. But wading is an excellent system, and you should be okay if you take care.

The third danger is more of a potential discomfort than any life-threatening problem. Hypothermia occurs when body temperature is lowered to a serious extent through having body heat drawn off into another medium. Most of the time, you'll be wading in water no more than waist deep, and it isn't a problem. However, avoid remaining in water so deep that your chest is submerged for long periods of time. A couple of hours in chest-deep water will leave you cooled down to a degree that you may experience discomfort.

Follows and Swirls

Now let's get back to the business of follows and swirls. They're a negative in that they indicate there was a fish following or interested in your lure, but not so much that it tried to eat it. The positive side is that the fish was interested in the first place. Now you merely need to interest it more. You know your choice of area was good; the fish are there. So was your choice of lure; the fish expressed an interest in it. The question is "Why was it not interested enough to eat the lure?"

There are several courses of action open to you, and they should be taken in the following order. First, change the speed of your retrieve. Slowing down or speeding up will effect two changes; it will alter slightly the action of the lure, and it will change the depth at which it is swimming. Either may be enough to trigger a hit.

If that doesn't work, try a lure of the same type, in a different color or combination of colors. It may be that your lure is imitating the action of normal prey, but isn't sufficiently close in color to convince your quarry it's good to eat. Perversely and frustratingly, it may also be that the lure too closely resembles normal prey. Apparently fish often want a bit of variety in their diet. For example, on the flats there are no baitfish normally found that are red and white with black spots. Yet MirrOlures in that color are one of the best lures on the flats. Once, when some fish were lying along the shore of the St. Lucie River's North Fork, but wouldn't hit, I tied on a yellow worm with black polka dots, resembling nothing I've ever seen. On the first cast, a fish nailed it, and I have a witness. Go figure.

Enhancers, covered in Chapter 9, were developed for just this problem. While many people think their purpose is to attract fish, it's actually to convince one already interested in a lure that the lure will be good to eat. While especially effective on jigs, enhancers also work with plugs, although they will have an effect on the action of smaller lures. If you don't have an enhancer on your bait, put one on. If you have one on already, be sure it's still fresh.

Still no luck? Change the type of lure. Here's an example of a frequent problem on the flats. Redfish have some difficulty in taking a lure on top, due to the placement of their mouth, which is not designed for surface feeding. Redfish can be taken that way, it just isn't their normal way of feeding, and many times they will follow a topwater plug but just not care enough to make a serious attempt at grabbing it. This will result in follows and swirls as the fish finally breaks off the pursuit, or it hits to the side or behind the plug.

It will also result in many failed attempts as a redfish tries to get the lure but misses, due again to the placement of its mouth and the attempt to modify its feeding habits. Quite often, switching to a jig, which is fished down where the redfish normally feed, will result in a hookup. This is so common that a long-time fishing buddy and I used it often to locate reds when they couldn't be sighted. We would alternate, one using a topwater plug, the other a jig. When the topwater lure attracted a red, the angler with the jig would cast it behind the topwater bait, frequently getting a hookup. After landing the red, we'd just switch jobs.

Does that mean a topwater plug trailed by a jig will frequently take redfish? Well, yes, as a matter of fact, it does.

Flats Fishing in a Nutshell

Okay, let's summarize this flats fishing business. First, scout a new area before trying it, if at all possible. Ease up to an area you'll be fishing as silently and unobtrusively as you possibly can. Best times to fish the flats are from just before dark, through the night, until shortly after full sunrise, but fish can be found on the flats any time. Work the deeper cuts and the holes, the edges of pockets in the grass, and the shoreline if that shoreline has something—like overhanging trees—that might cause fish to congregate.

Artificials are covered elsewhere in the book, but it's worth mentioning that some types work better than others on the flats. Use swimming plugs that run very shallow, topwater plugs, spoons, and jigs. Use the topwater plugs in lesser light and on overcast days, swimming plugs as the sun gets higher, or when you first start out if you're fishing sunset. Work jigs slowly, around the edges of holes and channels. An interesting lure for use where an ordinary lure might get snagged is the Solo, covered in Chapter 9.

Thar's Fish in Them Thar Trees

There's one more area of the flats that needs to be discussed, and that's the mangrove shoreline, one of the most productive grounds to be found for snook. There are two basic kinds of flats that offer this type of fishing; those adjacent to the shoreline, and those that extend out from mangrove islands.

Mangroves send down roots from their branches, and these comprise a veritable labyrinth in which crabs of several varieties, shrimp, and small baitfish find refuge, and in which redfish, snappers, and snook like to both feed and hide. It's quite amazing how shallow the water under a mangrove tree can be and still hold fish of a decent size. I've taken snook up to 20 pounds in 8–10 inches of water, enticing the fish out of the roots with surface plugs and jigs.

The trick to taking fish out of the mangroves is in getting the lure right up in the roots, as close as you possibly can. As a rule of thumb, if you don't snag a root or an overhanging branch from time to time, you aren't casting close enough to the trees. It's as simple as that. I know of no successful snook angler who doesn't get hung up from time to time. You *absolutely must* get your lure within inches of the roots if you're to be consistently successful in working mangrove shorelines for snook. There's just no way around it. If you're regularly dropping your plug two or three feet from the trees, you'll get snook, but only half or less of the potential number.

Branches that overhang the water, especially if there are two or more with open space between them, are holding places for snook. Remember what was said earlier about how fish that grow to maturity are those that pay attention not only to the water around them, but also to the sky. These branches give snook a feeling of security by protecting them from above. With relatively deep water beneath them, cover overhead, and nearby roots into which they can scoot for protection, snook like to lie around these overhanging branches.

The very thing that attracts snook to these shorelines represents the greatest deterrent to landing one, because a snook's immediate reaction to being hooked near the trees is to head straight back into the maze of roots in which it's always found both sanctuary and food. Your line, assuming it isn't cut by barnacles or other growths, won't last long rubbing against the roots, even with a leader.

The best way to avoid that is to use a somewhat heavier line than you would use out on the open grass flats, and put immediate pressure on the fish as soon as it's hooked, to pull it away from the trees. A relatively heavy leader of monofilament is an absolute necessity. You won't be able to turn all the snook that hit, especially if they haven't followed the lure out from the tree line 10 feet or so, but rather hit it right up at the roots, but you'll turn enough to make a difference.

If you can't turn the fish and keep it out of the trees, there are two things you can do. If you feel your line and leader are strong enough, you can simply try to drag the fish out by brute force. This isn't likely, but it may be worth a try. The second option is to remove all pressure, perhaps even by opening the bail on a spinning reel or taking a casting reel out of gear to give a few feet of slack. Many times, when pressure is removed, the snook will come back out on its own in an effort to leave the area, sometimes following the same path it did going in, especially if it hasn't gone in very far.

Sometimes.

An area often overlooked by people fishing around mangrove islands is called simply "the edge." This is for all practical purposes a ledge, although it may be less than a foot different in depth from the surrounding water. A good edge flows completely around an island, and will often hold fish, especially redfish and snook. Here's Captain Greenan on edges:

> "It's a kind of drop-off, and the edge is especially productive in those times when the water up in the mangrove roots is scarce. Frequently, the edge connects with holes around the island. The edge will follow, generally, the profile of the island. Don't be fooled by overhanging branches that may give the island the appearance of curving outward; follow the actual shoreline.
>
> "Where the edge curves in toward the island, it will frequently make what amounts to a bowl-shaped hole in the bottom. If large enough, this bowl will change the way the current flows past the island and bait will stack up in there. Snook and reds will lay around that bowl to ambush the bait. Edges are particularly productive at low tide or the beginning of the incoming."

Grass Beds

Strictly speaking, the miles and miles of grass beds found in 5 to 10 feet of water along both coasts, especially in the southern portion of the state, aren't considered flats, even though they have all the requirements but one; skinny water. The water is still relatively shallow, however, and you'll find many of the same species here that you encountered on the flats, although in different percentages. On the flats, redfish predominate, and from about midstate south are joined by snook and, in the extreme south, bonefish, cobia, permit, and tarpon. On the deeper grass flats, by far the species most often encountered is the spotted sea trout.

You may need some help in finding the holes and channels in this deeper water, but at the same time, they are less important than they were in the skinny water, as many fish simply cruise the grass or hide in it waiting for a meal.

Because sight fishing is the least productive method in this deeper water, we obviously must change our tactics. Using a quality sonar unit, you can still find those edges, cuts, holes and channels. Note the definitive "quality." If an inexpensive unit is going to be inaccurate in displaying depth, the problem is most likely to manifest itself in shallower water. Developments in design and manufacture have brought the price of better units well into the range of the average fisherman, and they should be given serious consideration if you'll be doing much fishing in water where the bottom isn't visible.

Adding a Global Positioning System (GPS) unit is also worth considering, because with the push of a button or two you can store the position of good locations so you can return to them later. (See Figure 5-4.) Inshore, landmarks will almost always be sufficient information for finding a previously located hot spot. But in the featureless country of the Gulf, for example, such landmarks may well be non-existent, or too far away to be reliable. A good GPS unit and sonar unit capable of reading small differences in depth will serve you well.

One of the most productive ways to fish these huge areas of grass flats is to simply drift over them under the influence of tides and winds. Swimming plugs that run at medium depths and jigs are good choices for artificials, and a popping cork with live shrimp or baitfish should call the fish to you from considerable distances.

Grass beds generally hold fish, so if you aren't getting hits, keep changing lures and colors until you find what they want. A positive attitude helps considerably when drifting the grass beds. Keep telling yourself the fish are there (they probably are), and that it's just a matter of finding what they want, and you should do quite well.

Fish, especially trout, on a grass bed tend to school, which means when you start getting hits or catching fish, it's a good idea to mark the spot. There are several devices available to do this. Most consist of a marker, line, and weight. When you reach an area you wish to mark, you simply toss the whole device over the side. The weight will unroll line off the marker, which floats, until

Figure 5-4. A global positioning unit, even a small one, will help you return to productive areas, especially in the featureless open waters of the Gulf, where landmarks are few.

it reaches the bottom. The line will stop coming off the float when the weight stops falling, and all you have to do is return to the marker to find where the school was holding.

The caveats of the flats also hold here in the deeper water. When returning to your marker, give it a wide berth and shut down your motor well upcurrent or upwind from it, and drift back. It will take a few more minutes to get to your marker, but there's more chance the fish will still be there than if you simply ran the engine right up to the marker.

The Marshes

Salt marshes are found along the Florida coast from about midway up the state all the way to the Georgia border and the Panhandle. Strictly speaking, many are not "flats," but they should be fished the same way, with one exception.

Salt marshes drain huge areas of grasses and muddy flats into shallow water, and frequently have at their head a river emanating from the interior of the state. Salinity will fluctuate with the quantity of rain in the interior, and this will have an effect on the species found there. There are many places where redfish and largemouth bass can be caught practically on alternate casts.

The channels and cuts that drain these acres of salt marsh also attract predatory fish eager to get in on the smorgasbord forced out of the marshes by a dropping tide. Work the mouths of these cuts, staying well off them if at all possible. Try to stay at maximum casting range, so as not to spook fish trying to feed at the mouths of these creeks. (See Figure 5-5.)

If using bait, place it in the current of the water coming out of the creek, preferably on one of the edges of the current. Artificials should be worked in an arc, starting at one side of the mouth and working through the center and all the way to the other side of the mouth. You should also try setting up on one side or the other of the mouth and working your lure across the outlet.

Jigs, tipped with a small piece of shrimp or an enhancer such as ProBait Tip-It are an excellent choice for working these creeks.

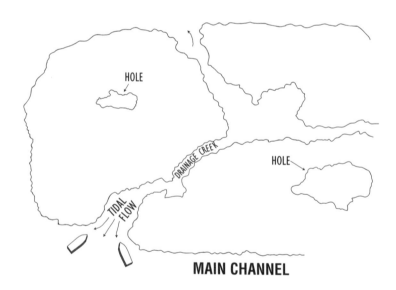

Figure 5-5. Fish the holes in a marsh on a rising or full tide; then work your way out, fishing the cuts and small channels as you go, finally positioning yourself at the main channel draining it.

Predominant species will be redfish, flounder, and trout, depending on season and the particular area of the state in which you find yourself. Five minutes' conversation in a local bait and tackle shop should tell you what you might expect to find at any given time of year.

Salt marsh areas should be scouted in the same manner as mud and grass flats; at low tide during midday. However, in most cases, you will be able to actually explore many of these marshes in much greater detail. This should be done on a rising tide, with full knowledge of the approximate time the tide will turn. Allow yourself a margin of error.

Work your way into the grass marsh on a rising tide, making maps to help you remember the many junctions of creeks, and showing your exact route into the marsh. Note especially where major channels are joined by smaller cuts that drain into the channels. These are the areas predators will work first, retreating back out of the marsh as the tide falls. Look back frequently; things look different from the opposite direction. (See Figure 5-6.)

No less than a half-hour *before* the tide is scheduled to reach its peak, start back out, using your map as needed. It's critical that you allow enough time, and don't dawdle on the way out. The last thing you want is to get trapped by a falling tide and be unable to navigate your way back out of the marsh. If that happens, you're stuck there until the tide returns enough for you to leave, and that could be as much as 12 hours. Biting insects and the surprising cool of Florida nights on the water will cause you a great deal of discomfort.

It's a discomfort, however, that's easy to avoid. Simply allow plenty of time and consult your map frequently. Note that in many cases, deep water may be only hundreds of feet away, may in fact even be visible. Yet the route to that water may be so circuitous that the total distance traveled is a half-mile or more.

Don't assume because you can see the bay or lagoon over the tops of the marsh grass that getting back to it will be a piece of cake. When exploring new areas, the smart outdoorsman errs on the side of caution. Always.

Figure 5-6. Marshes are home to incredible numbers of small marine life, such as crabs, shrimp, and small baitfish, nearly all of which must leave as the tide drops, using channels such as this one.

The Islands

Every now and then, you'll find an island completely surrounded by relatively deep water, as opposed to one sticking up in the middle of a grass or mud flat. Most support some sort of tree life, possibly mangrove, possibly casuarina (Australian pine), but many are bare. Some are covered even at low tide, although it may be by only a few inches of water. These islands should not be ignored, especially on high tides.

If the island supports mangroves, and the water under them is deep enough (a foot or more), the tree line is worth wading. But the most important part of an island to fish is the outer edge, especially on the spoil islands.

Spoil islands are created when dredged material is deposited on the side of a channel being dug. The most notable example of such a dredging project is the Intracoastal Waterway, and the best examples of those spoil islands can be found in the Indian River Lagoon, especially that stretch from Vero Beach to Jensen Beach.

In some cases, these deposits of dredged material don't even break the surface, except on the lowest tides. Others, as noted above develop extensive plant growth. Many are ringed by oyster bars.

Nearly all these islands are surrounded by deeper water, and the best way to fish these islands is to beach or anchor your boat and wade completely around the island, fishing as you go. If you don't find fish after one complete circuit, or at least see some signs of activity, go on to another spot. Fish aren't always around these islands, but they are a sure enough bet to be worth a try on any high tide. (See Figure 5-7.)

Skinny water fishing can be extremely productive, but you must pay the price, and that price is frequent scouting trips, studying the tides, learning to move stealthily, and putting in the practice time required to ensure accurate casts. Florida's underwater landscape is subject to frequent and sometimes major changes. Never assume a channel you negotiated easily six months ago is still deep enough for your boat, or that a new cut hasn't appeared

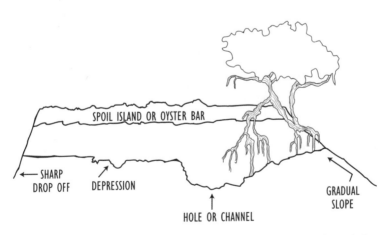

Figure 5-7. Spoil islands, oyster bars, and mangrove shorelines should be worked as thoroughly as time and tide allow, because they comprise a variety of underwater terrain.

in a bar. If you've been away from an area more than a few months, treat it as though you've never fished it before.

Fishing the skinny water is an exciting, novel way to catch fish, worth all the trouble. As a matter of fact, most skinny water anglers consider the scouting and all the pre-trip preparation an integral part of skinny water fishing, and you probably will, too. Because you're new to the state or to its inshore waters, the scenery and wildlife you'll encounter can only contribute to your enjoyment. Give it a try, and I'm sure you'll agree it's not only productive, but a great deal of fun.

And isn't that what it's all about, anyway?

Figure 5-8. Power Squadron and U.S. Coast Guard Auxiliary units both offer free inspections to ensure you meet all federal and state safety and equipment requirements.

What About
Those Beaches?

Florida has over 8,000 miles of shoreline, second among the states only to Alaska. Unfortunately for anglers, that doesn't equate to over 8,000 miles of fishing shoreline; much of it is either private property or is inaccessible from land. Nevertheless, it still means more fishable miles of waterfront than any of us has time to fish, and probably more than any other state.

Florida's shoreline is quite diverse in makeup. There are beaches with breaking waves typical of "normal" beaches, beaches with hardly any surf at all, grass-bed-covered shallows that go on for miles, coral reefs, and salt marshes. Whether you choose to wade casually with a one-handed spin rod, use a fly rod, or prefer to see how far you can fling six ounces of combined sinker and bait, it can be done in Florida.

Before I tell you how to catch fish from Florida's shores, allow me a bit of bragging rights. Dr. Stephen Leatherman, Director of the Laboratory of Coastal Research and Professor of Geography at the University of Maryland is known as one of the world's leading beach geologists. Each year, Dr. Leatherman examines 650 beaches throughout the continental United States and in Hawaii. He uses a rating scale that includes sand softness, water and air temperature, number of sunny days, currents, smell, pests, trash & litter, access, crowds, and crime rates.

St. Andrews State Recreation Area on Panama City Beach was selected in 1994 as the number four beach in the continental U.S. In 1995 it was rated number one, and we're proud of that. It's a great place to visit, and the jetty and piers produce some nice catches of fish, as Figure 6-1 demonstrates. Thanks for indulging me on this.

Figure 6-1. Mike Gogoe with one of a dozen nice sheepshead he caught from the jetty at St. Andrews State Park near Panama City using fiddler crabs for bait.

Surf Fishing

If you plan to fish from jetties and low sea walls often, you might want to get a long-handled gaff. If you can't find one, you can easily make one for yourself. All you need is some PVC pipe, some tape or clamps and a gaff hook. You may want to add a piece of dowel inside the PVC for stiffness. Bicycle hand grips make it easier to hang onto the gaff. (See Figure 6-2.)

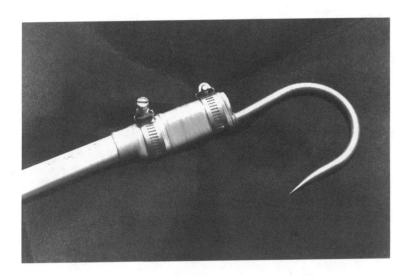

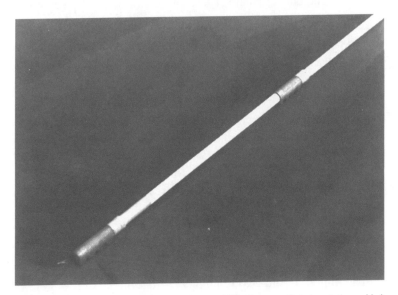

Figure 6-2. (a) I lashed the gaff hook to the PVC using waxed cord, and then added orange vinyl tape for low-light visibility and pipe clamps for strength. (b) A second hand grip halfway down the shaft aids in lifting larger fish, as does inserting a dowel inside the shaft for stiffness. Experiment with position before anchoring the grip.

Much of the shoreline, especially the Gulf and Keys beaches, can be worked very well from a small boat, but what we're interested in primarily in this chapter is what is typically thought of as "surf fishing." It's almost a certainty that the variety of species available to surf casters in Florida is unmatched anywhere in the United States.

First, however, although it isn't "surf" fishing, there is a kind of shore fishing available that shouldn't be ignored. Along both coasts you'll find barrier islands that offer easy access to the water on both sides. While the beach is the obvious place, don't forget the "other" beach; the side toward the mainland. On the east coast, for example, much of the Indian River Lagoon can be fished by wading as well as by boat, and the walk from your car to the water is in some places just a matter of a few feet.

The same holds true for the many causeways that connect the mainland and barrier island. These causeways may be an ecologic nightmare, but they do provide easy access and good wading.

To be successful at Florida surf fishing, it's necessary to understand a bit of what Florida's beaches comprise. Herewith, a brief primer.

There is a current that runs lengthwise down the entire eastern coast of the country, from New England all the way to the Florida Keys. Known as a littoral current, this water sweeps southward right along the coast, carrying with it sand, shells, bottles tossed in the ocean, bales of marijuana, etc. It's a long journey, and the littoral current, unlike many tourists, is in no particular hurry to get to Florida, and it isn't as consistent in its rate of travel as is, for example, the Gulf Stream. Thus, it may take as long as a hundred years for a grain of sand to move from North Carolina to Palm Beach.

The important thing to remember is that there is movement of water and sand in a generally southward direction along the coast. Waves and tides also play a part, assisting the littoral current at times, opposing it at others, which is one of the factors that govern the rate of sand transfer and the speed of the current.

Fishing the Sloughs

All this activity on the part of waves and currents, be they littoral or tide-induced, results in a quite uneven bottom immediately off the beach. Channels, called "sloughs," develop, running parallel to the beach for the most part, although there are some that run perpendicular to the shore, or nearly so. The sloughs that parallel the coast may be tens of yards long or may run for a half-mile. Occasionally, those running in toward and out from the beach connect those that parallel it, and the network can become quite extensive. Some are nearly as wide as they are long, and are referred to as "holes." (See Figure 6-3.)

Figure 6-3. Note the channels running parallel to the beach and also the depressions that form holes. The channels, called sloughs, and holes should receive extra attention.

The significance of these sloughs is that they're a veritable highway system used considerably by many species of fish, both prey and predator. While found on east, west, and Panhandle coasts, these sloughs are more noticeable, thus more easily found, on the east coast.

Fish those sloughs. It'll say it again, for emphasis: Fish those sloughs. And particularly, fish those sloughs *no matter how close they are to the beach.* One of the most commonly held fallacies of surf fishing is the farther out you can cast, the more fish you will catch. With some notable exceptions such as pompano, to which we will return, nothing could be farther from the truth, and the fish, in Florida.

While distance casting is a plus under such circumstances as fishing Cape Hatteras for channel bass, it's a waste of time for most species in Florida. I've caught redfish, snook, and tarpon so close to the beach in the wash that there wasn't enough water to completely cover the fish. That isn't usual, but neither is it rare, and snook will commonly cruise up and down a beach in a slough containing a foot or less of water. I recall once when Captain Greenan and I wondered whether or not the snook had sufficiently recovered from a cold front to be back along the beaches of Pine Island and Boca Grande. The water was clear, so we simply idled along the beach looking for them, in water so shallow the outboard's lower unit bumped the bottom several times. Because we weren't trying to catch them, just trying to see if they were there, we weren't concerned with spooking them. (Yes, as a matter of fact, they were.)

By casting straight out from shore and letting your bait simply rest on the bottom without knowing the actual configuration of the bottom at that particular spot, you're just hoping you've put it someplace where a fish will come across it.

Depending on blind luck, as it were.

On the other hand, casting directly into a slough increases the chance your bait will land in a place it's likely to be found and eaten. Whether or not a fish will actually find it is out of our hands, but at least you've put it where a fish will come along sooner or later.

The same holds true of artificial lures. Let's say just for the sake of illustration there are three sloughs within 100 feet of the wash, and they average 5 feet across. (Most are wider, to be sure, but let's keep the math simple for me.) You cast out to the farthest one and retrieve your lure, crossing each slough in turn. You cover 15 feet of potentially productive water and 85 feet of water that probably contains few or no game fish. In other words, your lure spent 85% of the retrieve where it was unlikely to produce. (See Figure 6-4.)

Casting 100 feet down a slough that's only 10 feet from the wash and retrieving your lure through that slough puts the ratio of productive to non-productive water at a minimum of nine to one; 90 feet to 10 feet. "A minimum" because many game fish such as redfish and snook are more likely to be found between the wash and the first slough than they are to be found between two sloughs

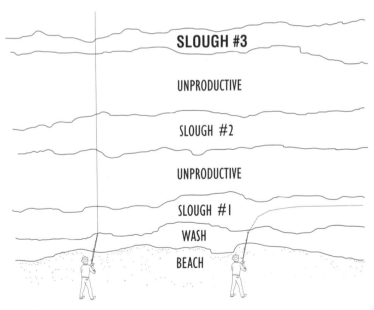

Figure 6-4. Sloughs are to fish what game trails are to deer, and should be fished thoroughly by casting parallel to them rather than going across them through primarily unproductive areas.

farther out. Because fish are frequently found right in the wash, before the first slough, using the second method increases the likelihood of a fish seeing your lure from slightly over 10% (because there's always the possibility a fish will be between sloughs) to near certainty, always assuming there are fish in the general area to begin with.

There are three easy ways and one relatively expensive way to locate sloughs. The expensive way is to hire a small plane and take some aerial photographs. The shading of the water will highlight the sloughs. A polarizing filter would be helpful. In some coastal counties, aerial photos (usually black and white) are available at the tax appraiser's office, and often are good enough to show at least major sloughs.

Locating sloughs and holes is most easily done at dead low tide, although it can be done at any tidal stage. Many of the close-in sloughs are completely exposed at low tide, long valleys of sand running parallel to the shoreline, and those that aren't are easily spotted by their lighter water color. That's the easiest and surest way to find them. If you can't make the trip at low tide, there are two ways to find them at higher stages. Many beaches have boardwalks or high sand dunes that will give enough elevation to discern differences in water color on calm days. That's one way, although not as sure as the first method. The final system requires the most experience, patience, and ability on your part, and that's reading the waves.

Reading the Waves

Breaking waves (except for those that are completely wind-induced, such as whitecaps) are created when a wave approaches the shallows of the shoreline. Water in a wave is moving forward, but at the same time moving in a circular pattern inside the wave itself. When it reaches the shallows, it becomes compressed into a smaller area and cannot retain its height. The circular motion within the wave causes it to fall forward over itself. Picture what would happen if you were running forward with your eyes closed and came to an unexpected upward slope; you'd trip. That's what waves do, in effect.

Frequently, before the water becomes shallow enough to "trip" the wave, it deepens again. This happens, for example, when an incoming wave encounters a slough. The deeper water allows the wave to stretch its height, and instead of breaking in a curl, it smooths out again. (See Figure 6-5.) This will happen, under the

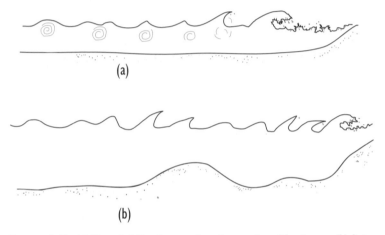

(a)

(b)

Figure 6-5. (a) Waves "trip" or "top-over" as they reach a rising bottom; (b) but a slough interrupts this action.

right circumstances, every time that wave encounters a slough of any significant size. The length of that portion of the wave that flattens out after beginning to break will indicate the length of the slough. If only a small portion of the wave fails to break, it's an indication of a simple depression, or a small hole.

Often, sand will build up on either side of a slough that runs perpendicular to the beach, creating what is in effect a mini-inlet leading into water deep enough to hold fish. These should be thoroughly tried, especially near the inlet, on both sides if possible.

Look for any obstruction—a reef or sand bar, for example— that creates a rip or eddy (circular, swiftly moving but not lengthy currents). This fast water makes for difficult swimming and maneuvering on the part of baitfish, giving predators the edge, and the predators know it. Live bait or artificials that can imitate struggling baitfish work well in these currents. Keep in mind that major storms or strong tidal currents frequently shift the location and depth of sloughs and holes. You'll need to reexamine the beach after such events to determine any such changes.

Likely Catches on Florida's Beaches

Now let's look at some specific species. Here's a list of those you're likely to encounter on Florida's beaches, and what you need to know to catch them.

Bluefish

While bluefish are migratory, a very small population does reside in Florida all year. As do so many visitors to Florida, they liked it so well they decided to stay. Most are quite small, and restrict themselves to inside waters such as the Indian River Lagoon or estuaries such as the St. Lucie River on the east coast, and shallows of the Gulf. During winter months, large bluefish (up to 20 pounds, in some years) follow the bait south and can be readily taken from the beach or from jetties and piers. While they do use the sloughs, blues will also range broadly along the surf, so don't restrict yourself to the sloughs. Blues are one of the exceptions to the rule of fishing close to the shore. Sometimes, distance casting is necessary.

Cut bait of almost any kind will take blues. Be sure to use a wire leader. It needn't be long, 6–8 inches, but you need to keep the bluefish's sharp teeth away from your vulnerable line. A 1/O hook should suffice. Use a large chunk of bait such as herring, mackerel, menhaden (pogy) and mullet. Blues are voracious eaters, and this is not the time to be sparing with your bait. Blues will also take shrimp, sand fleas, and live bait, such as white bait or small mullet and menhaden.

For artificials, it would be hard to beat spoons or "tin squids," such as the Crocodile, Kastmaster, or Hopkins lures. Keep them moving, and at a good pace. You cannot reel faster than a bluefish will swim to get a meal. Whichever lure you select, be sure to keep it shiny. As far as a bluefish is concerned, if something shines and moves, it's food. Tin squid lures offer an advantage over spoons in that they cast much more easily and farther, even into a stiff breeze, a not-uncommon occurrence at the shore.

Jigs also work quite well on blues, but the problem with using them is that the teeth of just a few blues will in all likelihood render the jig completely bare of hair or feathers, and a jig with a soft plastic tail is probably good for only one bluefish before the tail needs replacing.

Swimming plugs such as the MirrOlure are excellent for bluefish, but any lure used for blues should have its finish on the inside, visible through clear plastic. Wooden lures or plastic lures with a painted-on finish will lose their attraction quickly with frequent use for blues.

No matter which lure you use, a wire leader is a must, and shiny terminal tackle such as swivels should be avoided. It's not at all uncommon for a bluefish to strike a swivel, especially if it's being given "action" by a second, hooked, fish. Black is recommended, and leader wire should have a dull or bronzed finish.

Cobia

While not plentiful, cobia do occur at the shoreline, especially on the Gulf coast. Best baits are crabs, and the best lures are jigs or spoons. If the water is calm, look for swimming rays, as cobia will follow them in the shallow water, looking for crabs stirred up by the rays. Cobia are an extremely strong fish, and you should be certain to have a reel with a good and smooth drag, as you'll definitely need it. Don't try to horse a cobia in if you can avoid it, as you're more likely to break the fish off than you are to land one quickly. Cobia are frequently taken from long piers, such as the ones in Panama City Beach.

Flounders

Although flounders are found in the surf, if you're targeting them, you'll be better off fishing calmer waters on the east coast, those "beaches" previously mentioned on the barrier islands and causeways, for example. On the Gulf, it isn't a problem, as the surf is ordinarily not at all rough. Use live shrimp or live white bait. For lures, try jigs.

Jack Crevalle (Crevalle Jack)

Jacks cruise up and down the beach or shoreline, looking for schools of baitfish, which they promptly tear into. A school of jacks giving a working over to a school of baitfish, with the accompanying surface splashing, diving birds, and showering bait is a sight worth seeing. The incredible strength of jacks is testified to by the manner in which they swim through breakers. Especially during the summer, when they are most plentiful and the water is clearest, jacks can frequently be seen swimming through the curl of a breaking wave. Tin squids, spoons, swimming plugs, or jigs will all produce well on jacks.

Mackerel

There are three members of the mackerel family that can be caught from either the shore or some of the longer piers, although their numbers vary greatly, increasing during the summer months.

Cero mackerel. These medium-sized fish, running up to about 5 pounds, are rarely found far from south Florida, unlike the other two, which migrate northward each spring. Not commonly caught from the beach, but it does happen. Most caught inshore are taken from piers or boats. The yellow spots on their sides form a line above and below the lateral line. Only the cero has this line, running from pectoral to caudal fin.

King mackerel. It's rare to catch a king from the beach, but they are commonly caught from long piers that run into deep water. The largest of the three that concerns us, king mackerel run up to 20 pounds. There are generally thought to be two distinct populations, one in the Gulf and one in the Atlantic, with some mixing occurring from Key West to Cape Canaveral, in the winter. Young kings sometimes have yellow spots resembling those of

Spanish mackerel. A clue to identification, apart from the size, is the way the lateral line drops sharply at the second dorsal fin. **Spanish mackerel.** While Spanish mackerel also have yellow spots resembling those of the cero, the spots cover more of the side, and do not form the distinct line of the cero. The lateral line slopes in a gentle curve to the base of the tail. They school and migrate northward during the spring, returning to southern waters once the water temperature drops below 70°.

All the mackerels resemble bluefish in their roaming habits and food preferences. They will readily take cut bait, especially from the more oily fish such as mullet and, well, mackerel. Wire leader is recommended, and care should be taken in handling mackerel. King mackerel are known for leaping during the fight, and many an angler trying to boat a king has found himself with an unwanted boarder. Due to their size and strength, some sort of bridge gaff or bridge net is helpful in landing them from a pier.

Mackerel also share the bluefish fondness for lures that are both fast-moving and shiny. Spoons and similar lures will take all three types, the size of the lure coordinated with the species. Again, wire leader is recommended.

Of the three, Spanish mackerel are by far the species you're most likely to encounter from beach, bridge, or pier. In season (and all year 'round in parts of south Florida), they can be found along the beach, in bays and inlets, and in lagoons. Mackerel are schooling fish, and especially where cero or Spanish mackerel are concerned, it's unlikely you'll catch only one. Catching a mackerel is a sure sign there are more of them around. Because they work schools of baitfish at or near the surface, diving gulls and terns are a reliable clue a school of mackerel is in the neighborhood.

Permit

These fish are uncommon outside of south Florida, but they're included here because an opportunity to catch one of these great fighters should not be overlooked if you find yourself within their normal range, and they do occur at one time or another in most coastal areas of the state. Ranging up to 40 pounds, those inshore are generally smaller, although they may run as high as 25 pounds. Permit feed primarily on crabs, shrimp, small clams, and baitfish. Crab is generally accepted as the number one bait, and lures that can be worked to resemble a crab are best, such as jigs. There are artificials, such as those made by DOA lures, that resemble crabs quite closely, and fly patterns should do likewise. You'll find them inshore on grass and sand flats, in channels and, especially in the keys and the Gulf coasts, ranging sandy bottoms just off the beach.

Pompano

See, I told you we'd get back to pompano. As alluded to earlier, pompano don't spend much time close to the wash, preferring to cruise along sand bars and other high ground out in the deeper water of the beach, especially on the east coast. A long rod and a reel with high line capacity is a must for catching these tasty fighters on the east coast, while they will be found much closer to the shoreline in the keys and on the Gulf coast. East coast pompano fishermen regularly use rods of 11 feet or more. My personal choice for fishing for pompano from east coast beaches such as those found on Hutchinson Island is a 12-feet long rod mounting a Penn Squidder loaded with 20-pound-test line.

You may need as much as 4 ounces of sinker to hold bottom and to supply the weight for a long cast. Double-and even triple-hook rigs are favored by most pompano fishermen. Hooks should be 1/O or smaller, with a short shank. Monofilament hook leaders are sufficient, and some anglers add a piece of buoyant material to keep the hooks off the bottom, preventing the sand fleas from becoming covered by sand or actually burrowing in. I've always found it was sufficient to simply drag the sinker a few feet periodically.

Pompano have an endearing habit of striking so hard they generally hook themselves, and a frequent sight is a pompano fisherman gazing intently at the tip of a rod held in a sand spike, watching for the telltale twitching of a hit. Be careful about this; many counties have a limit on how many rods can be fished this way, so check first. Cast as far as you can, trying to get your bait on top of the outer sand bars, where pompano are rooting around for sand fleas, which should be your first choice for bait. If the fleas you're catching are small, simply use more than one on your hook.

Pompano migrate in the summer, and can be caught all the way up to the Panhandle. During cooler months, they are generally found below an imaginary line drawn across the state at about the southern edge of Lake Okeechobee.

For artificial lures, stay with jigs, primarily in yellow or yellow and white. Along the beach, most pompano caught on jigs are taken from small boats drifting along the coast, beyond casting range of the beach. However, they are commonly caught on jigs from bridges and piers.

Redfish

Although reds are caught from the beaches of Florida's east coast, it isn't as common as it is in more northerly areas such as the beaches on the Carolina barrier islands. When they do cruise the surf, it's generally close in, where they can pick up crabs and sand fleas. Most east coast reds caught in the surf are taken in or near jetties such as the one at Sebastian Inlet, where redfish in excess of 25 pounds are common. This doesn't mean you shouldn't try the beaches for redfish, only that there are more productive areas. On the Gulf side, redfish are commonly caught by those wading the shoreline.

Sheepshead

These can be caught just about anywhere in the state where there is a jetty. Fish close to the rocks using small hooks and fiddler crabs, with as little weight as you can. Small egg sinkers or split shot should be sufficient, as you aren't casting more than a few yards at most. These fish are quite adept at stealing bait, so be sure to have plenty on hand. Contrary to what an examination of their dental equipment might have you believe, sheepshead bite quite lightly, and you may miss many hits. Once you find the fish, if you don't get a bite within a few minutes, you might as well check your bait. Chances are it's gone.

Snook

I never kept count, but between the late '50s and 1989 I probably caught 1,000 or more snook from the beaches of southeast Florida. (Don't be overly impressed; one a week for twenty years would be over 1,000.) Of all those fish, I would guess 90% hit less than 50 feet from the beach. Possibly more, but I'm trying to be conservative. This point cannot be stressed too much, especially for those who are unused to the affinity of Florida fish for shallow water. If you simply cast straight out from the beach, most especially if you're using artificials, you ignore the most productive areas.

Snook will readily take cut bait, whole shrimp, sand fleas, and crabs. Use a generous portion on a 1/O to 3/O hook with a wire leader of 10 inches or more. (See Chapter 8 for the reasons.) An excellent bait for snook (unfortunately also a favorite of sharks and large gafftopsail catfish) is a whole mullet head, hooked through the eyes. Use a fishfinder rig for best results.

Cut mackerel, menhaden, mullet, and other typical cut baits will work well for snook, if properly placed. Dead shrimp will also do well, but stick with the larger sizes. For live bait, use very large shrimp, small ladyfish, small mullet (called "finger" mullet), small whiting, or menhaden. An advantage to using whiting is that you can usually catch them in the same places as you do snook, so a fresh supply of bait is readily available. Read on to learn how.

In artificials, jigs and swimming plugs will do the best job for you. The best jig colors are red, red-and-white, yellow-and-white, yellow, and solid white. Not necessarily in that order, so don't be shy about switching colors or color combinations, and don't restrict yourself to only those named.

Swimming plugs that have worked best for me over the years include MirrOlure, Rapala, Heddon and, most recently, some of the surface divers from Bill Lewis Lures. In the MirrOlure line, I prefer the 51M and 52M series, as they work a bit higher in the water, but the TT series also works well if you retrieve it fast enough as you approach the beach to keep it out of the sand. With the others, use floater/divers or shallow running plugs. Those that are designed to run deep will simply dig into the sand as you approach shore, or hang up on reefs.

As with jigs, combinations of red, yellow, and white work best, but the MirrOlure in green and gold should also be in your arsenal. For snook, plugs should be worked relatively slowly, and floater/divers should be allowed to come to the surface periodically. Twitch your rod tip from time to time during the retrieve, and while the lure is still out in the deeper water, allow it to settle a foot or so once in a while, then bring it back up by lifting your rod as you reel.

Surface plugs probably produce the least of all artificials in the surf on the east coast, as the water surface is usually not calm enough for proper action and visibility. On the Gulf shores, however, and anywhere else the water is flat much of the time, top water plugs will produce good results. The two that have worked best for me are the Zara Spook from Heddon and the Rebel Jumpin' Minnow. Large popping plugs will also work under the right conditions.

Color is least important in a surface plug, but you can't go wrong with the same combinations that work so well with the other types of artificials.

From first light until mid-morning and again from early evening to dark are the best times to fish for snook in the surf. While snook feed throughout the night, so do the sand flies and mosquitoes, a definite disadvantage from the standpoint of the angler. If you do try the surf during the night hours, be certain to protect yourself well with a good repellent.

Tarpon

As a general rule, tarpon are caught off east coast beaches only occasionally. Fishing for tarpon from the beach is marginally effective, as the tremendous runs of which they are capable leaves an angler rooted to the shore at a distinct disadvantage. Except for smaller fish, it isn't usually a high percentage endeavor. There are times, however, when landing a fish isn't the number-one priority; sometimes it's worth losing a big tarpon just to see it jump and carry on the way only tarpon can.

Those times come during the late spring and summer, when huge schools of mullet migrate down the coast, followed closely by equally huge schools of large tarpon. Long casts are the rule, but if you're capable of tossing a jig, spoon or tin squid two hundred feet or so, this is action you won't want to miss. Larger swimming plugs will also work well at times, but spoons seem to be the most effective.

Farther south, in the Keys, and up along the Gulf coast, small to medium tarpon are regularly taken by shore-bound anglers. On the Gulf coast, the preferred method is to work the shoreline with a small boat. During spring and summer, incredible tarpon fishing is available in the Boca Grande area by knowledgeable anglers.

Best bet for this fishing is to hire a guide. They know where the fish will be feeding and when, and the system used to take them requires a bit of experience and practice. Basically, one cruises the shore until moving tarpon are spotted. The school is carefully—and stealth cannot be overdone—carefully intercepted when they begin to "daisychain" and a bait—usually a live crab—is cast to a fish. Waiting until the tarpon has the crab in its mouth, the angler then sets the hook and hangs on during what is usually a long run. I once watched a large tarpon strip nearly three hundred yards of line from a reel before the engine could be cranked up to follow the fish.

Trout

These fish aren't generally taken from the surf on the east coast, but waders along the entire Gulf coast can expect good results. This doesn't mean you can't catch trout from the east coach beaches, just that it isn't the most productive place to try. If you do want to catch trout from the shore on the east coast, a much better bet would be to work from the shoreline of a barrier island, fishing one of the lagoons.

Weakfish, close relatives of redfish and trout that resemble the spotted sea trout physically, are regularly taken from Cape Canaveral north. Live shrimp are the number one bait for either trout or weakfish, followed by small white bait.

Surface (if water conditions permit) and swimming plugs will both work well for weakfish and trout, as will jigs and spoons. See Chapter 9 for more details.

Whiting

Small and unglamorous, whiting compensate by being ubiquitous, easy to catch, and quite good eating. Found from just beyond the wash to a couple of hundred feet from shore, whiting hit readily on cut bait, shrimp, or sand fleas, with the latter being the preferred bait. A little-known fact is that one of the best baits for whiting is whiting. Filet the first one you get and cut the filets into pieces about one to one-and-a-half inches square. Use a #1 hook or smaller on either single or multiple hook rigs. No leader is necessary. Not great fighters in the class of redfish, snook, or tarpon, whiting will nevertheless give a good account of themselves if not overmatched by heavy tackle.

No attempt has been made to include every species available from beach or Gulf coast, but those above are among the most frequently sought, and most often (with the exception of permit and tarpon) found in those environs. Other species likely to be encountered include several types of snappers, some members of the grouper family and the occasional odd black drum.

Chapter 7

Getting the Most from Your Boat

The main point I want to make about boats to be used for fishing inshore Florida waters is that it doesn't take much boat to do it. Advertising notwithstanding, you don't need a fancy glitter finish and upholstery worthy of a living room chair, you don't need mega horsepower, and you don't need a large boat. When I first started this type of fishing, it was with a 10-ft johnboat from Sears and a pair of oars. I replaced the oars after about a year with a 5-horsepower air-cooled Eska motor. After a couple more years, I graduated to a 14-ft aluminum semi-V hull by Starcraft, powered by a 25 Johnson. My son still uses that boat and motor, now twenty-some years old, and it still gets the job done.

Currently, I'm running a small (15 ft 9 in.) Renegade flats boat with 70 Yamahorses pushing it along, a poling platform, a 24-volt, 50-lb-thrust Great White trolling motor made by the MotorGuide folks, and a dual operation live well. I have an Eagle UltraNav combination Global Positioning System/depth finder, and a Humminbird VHF radio.

I've used canoes. I once tested a Grumman flat-bottomed boat with a Yamaha jet drive on it, for about a year, maybe more. I caught fish out of each and every one of those boats, and moving "up" was strictly a matter of comfort, not done to increase my catch. It increased my range, and allowed me greater variety of places to fish, but catching fish is a function of knowing where to go and what to do when you get there. It matters not how you arrived. (See Figure 7-1.)

In many cases, especially when fishing spoil islands or on the flats, the boat is simply transportation anyway. In the Indian River

Figure 7-1. it doesn't take much boat to fish inshore Florida waters. Even kayaks, which are surprisingly stable, can be used effectively with some modification, such as rod and tackle box carriers.

Lagoon, for example, I probably spend more than half my fishing time wading, and use the boat simply to get from one spoil island to another, or to move to a different part of the lagoon.

The point is that if it floats in shallow water and is a safe vehicle, it will get you to where the fish are in Florida. That being said, there is also the matter of comfort and of convenience, and if you want the very best flats boat available, and you can afford it, go for it. I sure would.

There are, however, a few requirements.

When I first began skinny water angling, boats specifically made for the purpose were pretty hard to come by, and the rules of economics allowed for few available variations. The few manufacturers who had shallow-draft boats offered a limited number of models, and you took what you could get. That's no longer the case. Today, there are many such manufacturers, and the variations are myriad. For that reason, I won't attempt to list what's available; I'm sure to leave someone out.

The common trait shared by all skinny water boats is, as might be expected, shallow draft, and that means draft measured in inches. If your boat draws much over a foot of water, there are many potentially productive places you'll simply have to avoid. Assuming that your boat is a shallow draft model, there are things you can do to make life easier for yourself, and add to your angling pleasure. If you're in the market for a boat, knowing what to look for might help you avoid a mistake you'll regret later.

If your boat has trouble getting up on plane quickly, it can be a problem. Often, especially in the backcountry, you'll have deep water for just tens of feet, before it shallows again, and those 50 or 60 feet are all you have to get up on plane. The alternative is to idle out until you reach deeper water. There is a possible cure for this, however, in the form of a hydro-foil.

There are several on the market, but I prefer the Doel Fin hydrofoil from the Doelcher Company, which is to the best of my knowledge not only the original, but the only one designed, as is an airplane wing, to lift the boat, as opposed to pushing it up from the bottom. Some boats, usually just a bit overpowered, sometimes poorly designed, will "porpoise," meaning the bow rises and falls at cruising speed, much like a porpoise sporting around. The Doel Fin will cure this problem in most cases. The Starcraft hull I mentioned earlier had this problem, as the engine was nearly too much power for the boat, and a Doel Fin cured it.

Accessories and Modifications

There are some things, of course, about which nothing can be done in the case of an existing boat, but there are ways around other requirements. Shallow draft, as we've seen, is a given. An extra-wide gunwale is a big plus, as it allows you to easily walk all the way around the boat while playing a fish, without trying to skirt obstructions such as coolers and tackle boxes.

There can be no such thing as too many rod holders, both those that hold a rod in the upright position (so-called "rocket launchers") and those that store the rods horizontally along the side of the boat. Yes, rods in rocket launchers do get in the way sometimes, and if you aren't used to them you'll probably hook one sooner or later on a back cast. However, after it's happened the first time and you've said all the appropriate cuss words and made reference to your own diminishing mental capacities, you'll begin to check for them automatically.

The convenience of being able to simply lift a rod and get a bait or lure into action quickly makes it worthwhile. The first time you see fish busting bait on top and fumble with holding straps or rod box lids only to find that when you finally do get into casting position the fish have moved on, you'll begin to use the rocket launchers. I don't pull away from a dock or launching ramp without a rod, usually rigged with a topwater plug, in one of the holders mounted on the side of my console, drag set, hooks checked, and ready for action. (See Figure 7-2.)

Consoles mounted in the center of the boat allow for ease in movement when fighting a fish, and keep your weight in the center if you're alone, but many people prefer a console mounted on the side. That's a matter of personal preference. A windshield on the console is a handy addition, not only as a windbreak for you, but also as a means of limiting the amount of spray that gets on instruments and electronic equipment mounted on or in the console's surface.

Sufficient dry storage is another must. Not only will there be days when you simply can't avoid spray, but there are nearly constant daily showers from June through November from which navigation charts, spare clothing, tools and so on must be protected. Check your storage areas and replace any gaskets that allow water to seep in.

Figure 7-2. Rugged Gear makes a Delrin plastic rod holder that comes with very strong suction cups and two means of permanent mounts. Use the suction cups until you know where you want the holders.

Electric trolling motors have made life on the flats much easier since the introduction of models resistant to the corrosive effects of salt water. You'll want the most powerful motor you can afford, preferably a 24-volt model. Don't feel, if your boat is relatively small, you can get by with a smaller motor, as the combined effects of wind and tidal current will quickly overpower a motor with insufficient thrust. While it's a nice addition, a propeller designed to cut through weeds is not generally required. Whichever electric motor you get, be sure to use deep cycle batteries and keep them charged.

A poling platform is a handy addition to any flats boat, even if you do have an electric motor. There will be times when it will be just as easy to pole a few strokes as to put the motor over the side, and other times when you simply won't want to risk spooking fish with motor noise. Fish on the flats spook for enough reasons we can't control, and we should reduce those we can. Never use a motor of any kind if you can see fish. If they're that close, don't take a chance with motor noise.

Another benefit to a poling platform is the added height it gives
you. There are two advantages gained by being up on a poling
platform. First, the added height allows you to see farther. Second, the sharper angle makes seeing through surface glare much
easier. The two combine to allow you to see both fish and obstructions farther off, giving you more time to take appropriate action
to either intercept or avoid, whichever is needed.

Check the space under your poling platform with the motor in
the raised position. If clearance is sufficient, you've just found
some previously overlooked storage space. I used mine to install
a PVC frame on which I mounted my VHF radio and a rack to
hold a tackle box. (See Figure 7-3.) The tackle box rack has
worked out very well, and I highly recommend it. It's best with a
box that opens from its face, allowing access to the contents without removing the box. I used a Plano Tackle Racker and, because
I don't have a security problem, the box rarely leaves its storage
space. The removable storage boxes make it a simple matter to

Figure 7-3. A holder for
tackle box, VHF radio and
other gear can be simply
fashioned using PVC pipe
and fittings, taking advantage
of any extra space beneath
the poling platform and
reducing clutter.

switch tackle if, for example, I want to fish freshwater, and the box is all plastic and can be washed with the rest of the boat after a day's fishing.

If your boat doesn't have a bait or live well with an aerator or water circulation system, consider the purchase of an add-on aerator or a large bait container with one built in. Live bait just will not last long without aeration, especially in the heat of a Florida summer day.

A good live well will keep your catch fresh right up until time to clean it. The well should have a pump and some system that refreshes the water when the boat is running without using the pump. Those in a round or oval shape, or at least with rounded corners, allow for the best water circulation.

A cooler as large as is practical should be aboard, and most of those available today are sturdy enough to provide an extra seat. Don't plan on being out on the water for more than a couple of hours without something to drink. The cooler in my boat is right in front of the console, making a handy seat that also keeps the passenger's weight in the middle of the boat, and I keep a plastic jug of water in it at all times.

You'll need some type of landing tool, either a large net or a gaff, preferably both. If you have no net, or if a fish is too large to land with your net, gaffing it through the lower lip will give you control over the fish, and if you want to release it, lip gaffing will do the least damage to the fish. It's also a handy way to control a fish while removing a hook, and allows you to leave the fish in the water and avoid any handling that will remove the protective slime.

There are, incidentally, some fairly good tools currently available to facilitate hook removal, and I highly recommend one in particular, called the Dehooker.

Some sort of cover, either a Bimini top or a full cover that can be folded down, is a nice addition. It will allow you to get out of the sun periodically, and provide a small amount of protection from rain.

If the boat is to be used for fly fishing, retractable cleats are a must. Fly lines, as do extension cords and measuring tapes, seem to have an uncanny knack for wrapping themselves around any available snag, and you certainly don't need a fish brought up short by a half-hitch around a cleat.

Be absolutely certain you have all the required safety equipment aboard. The Florida Marine Patrol is notoriously unsympathetic to boaters who ignore these requirements, as they should be. The regulations vary according to boat type and size, and may include any or all of the following: back fire flame arrestor(s) on carburetor(s); ventilation; personal flotation devices (in 1995, the requirement was changed to specify a *wearable* device for each person in any type or size of boat); bell or whistle (sometimes both); visual distress signals, and a fire extinguisher. If you want to learn the latest regulations that apply to your particular vessel, contact the Marine Patrol (see Appendix 1).

A good way to be certain you meet all safety regulations and requirements is to get a free safety inspection from a Power Squadron or Coast Guard Auxiliary unit. Both groups station members near launching ramps periodically for just this purpose, but you can get an inspection nearly any time by calling for an appointment. These groups are found throughout the state, and generally keep in contact with marinas in their area, so if you need to contact them, a marina is a good place to start.

A pair of polarized sunglasses will be a big help in seeing through the water to spot fish. You'll want sunglasses anyway, to protect your eyes from glare, so you might just as well get polarized lenses and see more fish. If you've never tried these glasses, do so. The difference will surprise you.

They're Closer Than You Think

One last word on using a boat in the inshore waters. Far too many people seem to be of the conviction that fish are always located "over there," "there" being someplace requiring a half-hour's running time. It ain't so. One of the blessings of my early inshore fishing was being forced to use a johnboat and a pair of oars. This limited my range, and made me explore very carefully places within easy reach of a launching ramp or a strip of unoccupied roadside where I could drag the boat to the water. I watched many an angler launch his boat and zip right past me, in a hurry to get "over there" where the fish were, while I was catching my limit within shouting distance of the ramp.

Here are just a few examples. On the east coast, just north of Fort Pierce, there is a launching ramp on the North Causeway that is right across a narrow navigation channel from extensive flats including Little Jim Island, Snapper Cut, and Jack Island. You can launch a boat there, paddle across the channel and drift with the tide across, literally, miles of productive water. Going just a bit farther, the very first spoil island north of the causeway is an excellent place to catch spotted seatrout, jacks, and snook. Hardly anyone bothers with it.

The same can be said about the Gulf Coast. Off Cedar Key, there are several grass flats within easy rowing distance that produce cobia, flounder, redfish, and trout; and there's a backcountry

Figure 7-4. Most coastal communities in Florida offer boating ramps, many with no launching fees. The Cedar Key ramp requires a fee but its excellent launching conditions make it worth the money.

ramp right in the heart of some of the best redfish territory in the state. (See Figure 7-4.)

The point being that the use of a boat can actually become counterproductive if you allow yourself to fall victim to the "over there" syndrome. By all means, explore far and wide. It's a good way to learn many spots to fish, a great way to see more of Florida's scenery, and it's fun. Just don't forget that, for someone at a distant launching ramp, "over there" is where you are.

Chapter 8

Specifics on Popular Species

For some species, you won't have to make major changes in your angling methods. For the most part, what you've used fishing for flounders in the northeast or trout and bass in freshwater can be applied. It's just a matter of knowing where and when, and what baits are best. I won't try to list everything that's available, just what you're most likely to encounter.

Bluefish

While migratory for the most part, there is a resident population of bluefish in Florida, mostly on the east coast. Most of these fish are small and the population is too small to make it worthwhile targeting them. You're more likely to come across them accidentally while fishing for trout, as they tend to congregate in the same places. During the winter, however, large schools of bigger fish are common.

East coast bluefish tend to be much larger than those in the Gulf. Three pounds is about the best you can expect on the west coast, whereas 20-pound fish are not uncommon on the Atlantic side during the winter migration. Bluefish tend to school by size, and rarely will you find a large bluefish with smaller ones or vice versa.

As they do elsewhere in their range, bluefish in Florida tend to move about quite a bit in schools. Blues are slashing predators, actively chasing their prey, unlike some species that lie in wait like the stagecoach robbers in a Tom Mix western. Often, the first sign of a school of bluefish is diving terns and gulls. If you aren't used to pelicans, learn to ignore them. Unlike the opportunistic gulls and terns, pelicans don't need feeding fish to hold their chosen meal in range near the top of the water. Diving pelicans do indicate baitfish, but don't necessarily mean something is under that bait.

Most blues are taken on the east coast from beaches or jetties, or from a boat. Schools definitely will come into such bodies as the Indian River Lagoon or Lake Worth, on occasion holding in one section if it's worth their while. In the Fort Pierce area, for example, blues will frequently come in through Fort Pierce Inlet, move north a mile or so, and hold at the mouth of Taylor Creek, especially on a dropping tide. Similarly, blues coming in St. Lucie Inlet will hold in the deeper channels on the flats just north of the inlet.

Blues prefer large chunks of oily cut bait, such as mackerel, mullet, or ribbonfish, and all good bait shops generally have a good supply during bluefish season. The real ribbonfish is a member of the drum family, and most of the bluefish bait sold as ribbonfish is actually Atlantic cutlassfish, but it's still one of the best baits, by any name. Don't be stingy with your portions, as the emphasis is on "large." A 1/O hook and short piece of wire leader in a dark color should be used, and the bait fished on the bottom. Don't use bright leader wire or terminal tackle, as blues will bite it, especially when it's moving; as when you're reeling in a hooked fish. Some anglers use a piece of foam or cork to hold the bait a few inches off the bottom to discourage crabs from getting to it.

If fishing from a bridge or pier, try to fish where the current is moving well, as blues tend to find the moving water. The same holds true for boat fishing. Look for the deeper, fast water of inlets, estuary outlets, and the channels of the ICW.

In artificials, shiny is best. Blues are of the conviction that if it shines and it moves, it's food. Spoons and "knife-handle" jigs, such as the Hopkins, work very well for blues. Swimming plugs will also work well, especially those with a bright finish. Color is less important to bluefish than to other species. As with bait, use a short piece of wire leader in tobacco or another dark color.

Bluefish tend to die quickly after being caught, even when placed immediately into a live well, so a cooler full of loose ice is a better choice for storage until the fish can be cleaned.

Cobia

These are also called ling, especially in the Panhandle area. Although primarily an offshore species, cobia do frequent inshore waters, especially during the warmer months. You'll find them around buoys, channel markers, reefs, and wrecks, but also on the flats, especially on the west coast, and smaller fish are found even in mangroves. From above, looking down at a cobia's back, the first impression is "shark." Cobia are long and slim, built for speed, and very strong swimmers.

Their primary foods are small fish, squid, and crabs. When on the flats, cobia are fond of following along behind rays and manatees in search of something edible disturbed by the larger animals. A wandering ray or manatee is always worth an exploratory cast or two. While crabs will take cobia, most anglers use artificial lures, with jigs and spoons the preferred choices.

Don't try to horse in a cobia. As stated, they are extremely strong fish, and when you hook one you might as well plan on being there a while. Let them run and let your tackle do its job, and you'll land most cobia you hook. Try to force the issue and chances are you'll end up with a break-off.

Flounder

Flounders are bottom-dwellers, preferring to lie in wait for their food, sometimes covering themselves with a thin layer of sand or mud, sometimes relying more on a mottled camouflage for concealment. There are three species found in Florida, all in different parts of the state, although there is some overlap of range. All three feed primarily on small fishes and crustaceans, and will readily take shrimp. Use small hooks, nothing larger than a number 1. Although some are taken in grass beds, they prefer mud or sandy bottoms.

Jacks

There are many members of the *Carangidae* (jacks and pompanos) family represented in Florida, but the one most people mean when they say "jacks" is the jack crevalle, or crevalle jack. Jacks readily take baits such as small fish or shrimp, but by far the preferred method is artificials. Food value is negligible, so most are released. Jacks are voracious feeders, cornering schools of baitfish at the surface or against sea walls in a spectacle that can be seen at great distances.

They will hit all types of artificial lures, from jigs and spoons to both topwater and swimming plugs. Extremely strong, they don't give up easily, and will commonly make several long runs. Using tackle that isn't up to the job will, unfortunately, cause many jacks to literally fight to the death, so be prepared to break off a fish too large for your tackle.

Having caught a few jacks, you will quickly learn to recognize the powerful runs and the vibrating, throbbing fight that characterize their method of doing combat. Common to about 5 pounds inshore, jacks in the ocean can exceed 30 pounds. They are found throughout the state, and are extremely tolerant of varying salinity, frequently roaming far up drainage canals, estuaries, and rivers.

Mackerel

Although they are often caught inshore during the summer months, especially from long piers in the panhandle area, king mackerel (usually called "kingfish") are primarily an offshore species, and won't be dealt with here. More common are the cero mackerel and Spanish mackerel, with the smaller Spanish more common by far, as the larger cero tends to stay in the southern part of the state.

The two can be distinguished most easily by the yellowbrown stripes that run from pectoral to caudal fin on the cero, replaced on the Spanish with yellow spots.

Most mackerels are schooling fish, and these two are no different. Spanish mackerel prefer water at least 70°F, and migrate northward during spring. During the winter months, schools of mackerel range over grass flats, through channels and along the beaches.

Primary foods are fish and squid. Mackerel can be taken on cut bait or artificial lures, spoons being the best choice. A wire leader is recommended.

Pompano

Another *Carangidae,* the Florida pompano is found primarily in the southern part of the state during most of the year, but migrates up both coasts during summer months. While seasonal movements are controlled by temperature, local ranging is dictated by the tides, as they move onto sand and oyster bars to feed. Pompano are a favorite target of Florida surf-casters, and are most commonly caught along east coast beaches. Long casts are the norm, as the fish are generally out beyond the first sand bar. They feed primarily on sand fleas, but will also take small crabs and pieces of clam.

Pompano have a "soft" mouth, and a leader is not needed with lures. The best choice for artificials is unquestionably a jig, preferably yellow or yellow-and-white. Let the jig go all the way to the bottom and retrieve it with a lifting motion of the rod, bouncing the jig along the sandy bottom. An excellent way to catch pompano is to drift in a boat a quarter-mile or less off the beach, especially in the area from Indian River County to Palm Beach County, using a yellow jig. Let the jig go all the way to the bottom and bounce it along, lifting the rod tip at least a foot. Be prepared for a hard strike, which will generally come as the jig falls back toward the bottom.

Most surf-casters prefer to stay with sand fleas, as it's generally impossible to cast a lure far enough. Pyramid sinkers as heavy as 3–5 ounces may be needed to hold the bait in the current. As there are frequently coral and limestone or worm rock reefs near where pompano feed, many anglers attach the sinker with a short piece of leader of lesser breaking strength than their fishing line or hook leaders, so they can break off a stuck sinker and leave it, while retrieving their line and hooks. Three-way swivels are generally used.

Multiple-hook rigs are common, most often three #1 hooks tied on monofilament. Pompano hit quite hard, and it's rarely necessary to set the hook. Many pompano anglers cast far out onto a sand bar and simply set the rod in a sand spike and watch the tip for the vibrations of a hooked pompano.

A trick used successfully by many is to wade out as far as is comfortable, cast, let the bait sink to the bottom and close the bail or put the reel in gear. On the walk back to the sand spike, drag the sinker in the sand, gouging a trench that many feel lures a pompano to the bait.

They are strong fighters, using their broad bodies to add resistance in the water, and are capable of long runs.

Pompano are high-strung, if such a phrase can be applied to fish. This is evident in the frantic behavior exhibited as a hooked fish approaches a boat or shore, and in the darting, almost frenzied way a pompano will exit shallow water when startled by a boat, sometimes even becoming airborne.

Pompano are considered by many to be the epitome of fine eating, with firm, rich flesh. They are delicious prepared many ways, but especially broiled.

Red Drum

If any species of fish found in Florida can be called ubiquitous, this is it. There are literally no geographic sections of the state in which they are not found. Most commonly called a "redfish" or simply "red" in Florida, these fish also go by the name "channel bass," especially north of Georgia. Although there is a definite reddish cast, redfish flash bronze when moving on the flats, and that's frequently the first sign for an angler poling the flats in search of them. Reds inhabit the inshore areas until they reach spawning size of about 30 inches at about 4 years of age, when they migrate through the inlets and passes to spawn offshore.

Coupled with their strength, the size of redfish demands quality tackle. Good line, a rod with backbone, and a reel having a strong, smooth drag are absolutely required. A redfish of 27 inches, the largest that can be kept at this writing, will weigh roughly 8 pounds, but often an 18-inch red will feel like it does.

The mouth of a redfish is horizontal and opens downward, a good indication of its primary food source of crustaceans and mollusks, although reds do eat small fish. Because of the location of the mouth, reds have a difficult time striking a topwater plug, and that's the least effective way to fish for them, although it's an excellent way to locate them. Reds will come from a good distance to locate the source of a surface disturbance, and often make an attempt to grab the plug.

Two anglers, one with a topwater plug and one with a jig or spoon, can thus lure reds into range and present the underwater lure. This is not to say reds can't be taken on topwater plugs; they can and are. There are just many more efficient ways to catch them.

Redfish prowl the flats, cruise up and down the beach, move over oyster bars and search the cuts and channels for a meal. Very large reds are taken in the deeper waters of inlets and passes, and Sebastian Inlet, approximately halfway between Melbourne and Vero Beach on the east coast, annually yields many fish of 25 pounds or more, most taken on cut bait, but some on jigs and even a few on swimming plugs.

Reds, infrequently single fish but more often groups or small schools, move up onto the flats with the rising tide, moving across them looking for crabs, shrimp, and small fishes. From time to time, huge schools numbering in the hundreds congregate, ranging across the flats like some huge undulating monster and turning the water copper-bronze as they flash in the sun. It's a sight not often seen, but if seen, never forgotten.

Although reds will get up into the mangroves, that's not their preferred hunting ground. Look for them around oyster bars and on the grass flats near sandy patches. Around mangrove islands, reds are more likely to be found at the edge than in the tree roots. (See Figure 8-1.)

Sight fishing for reds can be quite productive once you learn what to look for, and provided you have a good pair of polarized sunglasses. As are all fish in the skinny water, they are easily spooked, and you should take care to avoid any unnecessary noises such as scraping tackle boxes or dropping items on the deck.

Preferred live baits for reds are shrimp and small white bait such as mutton minnows and crabs. Popping corks work well for redfish. Redfish have a tough mouth that calls for sharp hooks and a positive hook set. They have teeth that are all but insignificant by comparison with many other species, but don't be fooled. They are there, and larger fish should be landed with a net, although small reds can be safely lifted with a thumb in their mouth ála largemouth bass and snook.

On any given day the best artificial for redfish will generally be either a spoon or a jig. In the absence of any sign such as particu-

Figure 8-1. Captain Greenan with a redfish (red drum) that took a Greenan Redfish Fly in the backwaters of Bull Bay, a part of Charlotte Harbor in southwest Florida.

larly clear or especially muddy water, you can safely decide which
to use at the start of a day's fishing by tossing a coin; you'd be right
more than half the time. Many anglers prefer silver spoons of various brands for reds, but I've had my greatest success using a gold
Johnson spoon, with the color more significant than the brand.

With jigs, dark heads such as maroon seem to work best under
conditions generally encountered on the flats, with soft plastic
tails in darker colors—maroon, black, red, and so on. If the water
is particularly murky, switch to a light-colored head and a tail of
yellow or chartreuse. I've also enjoyed great success with both
pink and purple tails.

I asked Captain John Kumiski, guide and the author of *Fly
Fishing in Florida,* for his favorite flies for various Florida gamefish, and here are his choices for redfish: 1) Clouser deep min-

Figure 8-2. Larry
Larsen holds a redfish
while Capt. Van Hubbard
prepares to insert a tag
prior to releasing the
fish, one of hundreds the
guide has tagged for
tracking.

now; 2) Fuzzy crab; and 3) Seaducer. I would also add the Greenan redfish fly, Captain Greenan's own creation.

Greenan's first choice would be—drum roll, please—his own Greenan Redfish Fly, followed by a popper in red and white, a Clauser Minnow in chartreuse, black or gray, a brown and olive crab fly, and a tan shrimp fly, all tied on #1 hooks.

Released redfish will sometimes go straight to the bottom and lie there, belly up, appearing for all the world to be dead. Don't despair. Boca Grande Guide Chris Mitchell once showed me a great trick for use on these redfish. Taking his push pole, he reached down and gently touched the fish on its exposed underside. The red immediately righted itself and darted off, obviously healthy. I've seen him do this several times, and have used the trick on several occasions myself. I don't know why some redfish have this propensity for playing dead, but it's always a relief to see the fish swim off after a gentle nudge, and it's worked every time for me.

Snappers

There are more than a dozen species of snappers found in Florida, from the monster cubera to the diminutive queen snapper. While the cubera can reach weights in excess of 100 pounds, and most others such as the red snapper are common up to 20 pounds, most of the snappers caught inshore are under 3 pounds. This is due as much to the fact that many are juveniles of species that spend most of their life offshore as it is to inshore snapper species being primarily smaller fish.

Nevertheless, snappers can give a good account of themselves if you match your tackle, and are great sport on light or ultra-light tackle. Most like to hang around cover of some sort, so they are frequently found near mangroves, bridges, and floating docks. You'll also find them in grass beds and on the flats where grass is dense and high. Most small fish don't like to be far from some sort of cover, and snappers are no exception.

In the early 1980s, snappers were in big trouble, with the number of fish dropping at an alarming rate. In 1986, however, the Florida Marine Fisheries Commission placed in effect strict new regulations, comprising a 5-fish bag limit and a 10-inch minimum size, which resulted in a marked increase in the number of snappers in Florida waters.

By 1991, according to Mike Murphy, a marine research scientist with the Florida Department of Natural Resources, the recreational catch of snappers had gone up nearly 100%. In January 1995, the minimum size was increased to 12 inches, and that's expected to augment the spawning population even more. Consequently, prospects are good and getting better for not only more snappers, but larger ones. Although the size increase will be more noticeable in adult fish taken over the offshore reefs, snappers in the 4-pound range are now being taken routinely in Gulf Coast inshore waters.

Because more than one species of snapper may share a given hideout and their diets are so varied, the type of bait you use is next to irrelevant. For example, gray snappers, more often called mangrove snappers, juvenile mutton snappers, and schoolmasters can all be found inshore and all feed on crustaceans and small fish with the occasional snail just to balance things off. Every species of snapper found in the inshore waters will jump on a live shrimp like a chicken on a June bug, and all will also take cut pieces of dead shrimp or fish. There are few less-fussy eaters than the snapper family, especially in the smaller sizes, and they all have appetites that can only be described as voracious. Use small hooks, #2 or smaller.

You won't need sophisticated tackle either; a cane pole and bobber will do. Not that these fish can't fight. A snapper of any kind on an ultra-light outfit will provide great fun. The reason many people don't realize this is that snappers inshore are so frequently caught incidentally on tackle designed for much larger fish. Try ultra-light tackle for snappers and be pleasantly surprised.

Ultra-light is also about the only way to take small snappers on artificials, as the lures must be so small and light it's virtually impossible to cast them with ordinary tackle. Try light and bright jigs of the type sold for freshwater panfish, such as crappie, and jig them over grass beds and around mangrove branches and roots.

Snook

Ah, yes, snook. My personal favorite, both for the fight they give and for the methods by which they can be caught. Not incidentally, they're also one of my favorites on the dinner plate. I moved in 1989 from southeastern Florida to north-central Florida and my only regret is that snook don't come as far north as the Cedar Key area, which is about as far south as I fish on a regular basis. You can bet, however, that any business that requires travel to the southern part of the state also provides an excuse to get in a bit of snook fishing.

There are actually four types of snook in Florida, but you aren't likely to encounter three of the four.

Fat Snook. These have the deepest body of the four, hence their name. Rarely more than 20 inches in length (although a new IGFA all-tackle record fish of 7 pounds, 4 ounces was caught at Jupiter, on Florida's east coast, by Theodore Barrick in November of '94), the fat snook is commonly found in fresh water and occurs more in interior waters than the others. Mangrove shorelines serve as nurseries, and some adults are also found there. Yellow-brown to green-brown on the back and silver on the sides, they lack the darker outer edge on the pelvic fin (that's the one farthest forward, on the bottom, also called the ventral fin), and it has the smallest scales of any snook.

Swordspine Snook. This fish derives its name from the very long second spine on the anal fin (rear most on the bottom). It's the smallest of the snooks (although ironically has the largest scales of the four), generally 12 inches maximum, and weighing less than a pound. They aren't found everywhere, coming only to about the North Fork of the St. Lucie River on the east coast, and are rare on the Gulf side. Like the fat snook, they prefer fresh or only slightly brackish water.

Tarpon Snook. Another small fish that at its maximum will barely reach the minimum keeping size for snook (currently 18 inches) and, like the swordspine, generally less than a pound. It, too, is rare on the west coast.

I stated earlier that you would probably never even encounter any of these three species. To put it in perspective, of the thousands of snook I've caught, I doubt more than three dozen have been fat, swordspine or tarpon snook, and nearly all of those were caught in the St. Lucie River. But now we come to the big guy.

Common Snook. This is the largest of the snooks, with a distinctly divided dorsal fin, a sloping head ending in a mouth that could hide a small car, a yellow pelvic fin (farthest forward, on the side) and the most distinct black lateral line of all four species. Much to my dismay, they can't tolerate water much below 60°F (59°F is usually given as minimum water temperature). They can tolerate completely fresh water, but much prefer saltwater.

The snook population in the Cape Canaveral area took a major hit during a hard freeze a few years back, along with much of the mangrove growth. Fortunately, things are looking good for the future, and a fair number of snook have already begun to show up. Enough, at least, to make a trip for snook worthwhile.

Figure 8-3. This snook thought a Cotee jig would make a pretty good meal. Even small snook get acrobatic when hooked and put on quite a show on light tackle.

Common snook school along shore and in inlets and passes during spawning season, which is the reason the snook season is closed during summer months. (It's closed during January and February because cold spells frequently make snook lethargic and therefore easy prey to unethical "anglers" who snag them with jigs or large treble hooks.) Although snook of 40 and more pounds in weight are not unheard of, most caught inshore are more likely to be under 15 pounds.

Larger snook—20 pounds or more—generally confine themselves to the inlets, passes, and beachfront shorelines and deeper waters such as are found near some of Florida's bridges over the ICW. Feeding on crabs, white bait, and larger baitfish such as mullet and small members of several forage species as well as shrimp, large snook can be taken on any of those baits. They will also hit large swimming plugs and jigs, feeding mostly at night. Fish for them from jetties and bridges, especially where lights shine onto the water, attracting small fish and shrimp, and where the lights cast a shadow on the water. A bridge gaff or bridge net is a definite requirement.

When conditions allow and a bridge isn't too crowded, the best method is to cast parallel to the bridge, working your lure at the edge of the shadow line. Snook can often be seen lying at the surface under the bridge, facing in to the current. (See Chapter 4.)

While the occasional snook over 20 pounds will be taken in the skinny water, most are smaller, as was pointed out above. Given that, most of what follows deals with the smaller, more commonly found snook.

If bluefish and mackerel are slashing raiders, and redfish are foragers, snook must be considered the muggers of inshore waters. They are prone to hole up in mangrove roots, on mangrove island edges, in the holes on flats, around pilings and under docks while waiting to ambush Meals On Wheels. They also will do a bit of prowling, especially on the grass flats, but much prefer to have their food come to them. Snook are far more active feeders on incoming tides than on the outgoing. On the flats, preferred foods are baitfish, shrimp, and crabs. I rarely use bait for snook, so I went to the experts for their opinions. Here's what Captains Pete Greenan and Ben Taylor had to say.

Greenan: "White bait, preferably scaled pilchards, about 4 to 5 inches long, or hand-picked large—I mean very large—lively shrimp. Third choice would be a grunt about 5 inches." Also good are small ladyfish, pinfish, or lizardfish. I wouldn't insult a snook by offering it cut bait."

Taylor: (1) The smallest pinfish I can find, hooked through the eyes so it can't be stolen easily; (2) finger mullet hooked far enough behind the upper lip so they don't come off during the cast, hook facing up; and (3) a big shrimp hooked just in front of the brain." (The brain, you will recall from Chapter 3, is the dark spot visible in the head.)

I also asked John Kumiski, guide and fellow writer from Florida's Space Coast up near Cape Canaveral. He said his favorite live bait for snook is a large white streamer fly. Hmmm. Never got any in my cast net.

Snook will readily take many types of artificial lures. On overcast days, preferably with just enough wind to keep the surface disturbed, and preferably very early or very late in the day, it would be hard to beat a topwater plug for snook. I've had the most success with a Heddon Zara Spook, but there are many others that will work quite well, including the Rebel Jumpin' Minnow and various popping plugs such as the Pop'R, the Chugger Spook, and a new offering from Bill Lewis Lures called the Spitfire.

Injured minnow lures with propellers such as the Devil Horse or the Heddon Dying Flutter will work for snook, but they generally prefer a lure that's more subtle. Especially under the poor light conditions of pre-dawn and half-past sunset; the color does not matter much, but during daylight hours it will pay to experiment a bit. Because poor light gives the fish more of a silhouette than a side view as with a swimming plug, black does seem to have a slight edge. In full light, start with the old standby red-and-white and work your way through yellow, white-and-yellow and chrome, all the way to black.

Many swimming plugs are effective on snook, but few will beat the long-time favorite of Floridians, the MirrOlure. Use

Figure 8-4. Capt. Greenan was kind enough to hold my snook for a photo after it decided a Zara Spook was making entirely too much commotion. The fish was exactly the maximum size for keeping.

medium sinkers such as the 52M series, in red-and-white, gold-and-white, or gold-and-green for starters.

Jigs with a dark head—red or black—are favorites among snook fishermen, usually used with a root-beer or motor-oil-color tail. If the water is murky from sediment or is stained by tannin, use brighter colors such as white or yellow for the head, and a tail of chartreuse, bright pink, purple, or even white. If you choose something multi-colored such as a white tail with a red or orange tip, be prepared to lose some tails, as sailor's choice, pigfish, and other small baitfish love those brightly colored tips and will frequently bite them off.

I've had a good deal of success under poor light and water conditions with a white jig and a chartreuse tail. The beauty of jigs with plastic tails is in being able to experiment with different color combinations, so don't be afraid to be a free spirit.

A favorite of mine is the Cotee Rattlin' Liv'Eye jig, which has a plastic head filled with small shot and a lead collar that slips over the hook before the tail is put on in order to adjust the weight of the jig and, consequently, the depth at which it will run.

White streamer flies get the nod for fly casters, large, full flies with good breathing action in the water. As with plugs, yellow, yellow-and-white and red-and-white are also good choices, and don't forget the darker colors, which work well under the right conditions.

Again, here are the experts' opinions on flies:

Greenan: "A Finger Mullet pattern in red and-white, then a Greenback Finger Mullet, a Greenback Deceiver, a chartreuse-and-white Deceiver (yellow in water stained by tannin), a Clauser and for fishing around lights at night, a pearl Glass Minnow."

Kumiski: "(1) Large Deceivers, (2) Rattlin' Minnow, (3) either a large hair bug or a Seaducer."

Snook have very fine teeth, almost like sandpaper, which in combination with the sharp edges of their gill covers means you'll need a leader. Wire will work, but most prefer to use monofilament and simply cut it back when it becomes abraded, which won't take long. Start with a leader of at least 18 inches if you choose monofilament. With wire, 8 inches will do.

An advantage to a snook's dental equipment is that it makes it not only possible but practical to land smaller snook by simply inserting a thumb in their mouth and clamping the lower jaw between thumb and forefinger. You can easily lift the fish into the boat or carry it to shore. Be very careful of the bottom edge of the gill plate, as the sharp edges alluded to earlier can easily inflict a nasty cut to a finger.

If you plan to release the fish, you can generally hold it in the water while you remove the hook. Larger fish are best landed with a net or gaff. If you have no net, or the fish is too large for your net, gaff it through the lower jaw and hold it in the water just as you would hold a smaller fish with your hand.

Snook are extremely powerful swimmers, and think nothing of charging into very swift water after smaller fish that are rendered all but helpless. I'll illustrate with an anecdote. I can't tell you the location, simply because it's a place where only one, or at the most two anglers can fish at the same time, and I want to be fair to the man who tipped me off to it, but this has to do with a place that is as sure-fire as they get.

On very specific conditions; fully dark, very strong (15 knots or more) northeast to north winds and a strong incoming tide (which in this place would be opposing the wind), the water races under a bridge and is whipped into whitecaps by the wind. A person can wade into the water and cast a red-and-white 52M Mirr-Olure downcurrent, letting the tide sweep it toward the bridge, and catch a snook on about every tenth cast. The current next to the bridge is so strong, it's all a body can do to keep his feet. I've been nearly knocked down several times. The water is roiled and choppy, and it appears nothing would be able to swim in it, but the snook are there, actively feeding on smaller fish nearly helpless in the current.

A very strong fish indeed, the snook.

Tarpon

The best advice for newcomers who want to catch a tarpon, especially a large one, can be summed up in one very short sentence: Hire a guide. While tarpon can be found throughout the state at one time or another, they can be finicky feeders, wanting one thing one time and something entirely different another, and they require tackle far heavier and more specialized than other inshore fish. Consequently, for these reasons and others, it would be wise to fish with a good tarpon guide, at least the first few times.

I'm not hedging on my advice, but if you can't hire a guide and want to try it on your own, here's how to go about it.

By far your best bet is to concentrate on smaller tarpon in the backcountry, in the same areas you might expect to find redfish and snook. When feeding, tarpon will readily take live bait and artificials. The key word is "when." Few things are more frustrating in the angling world than finding tarpon and watching them roll lazily at the surface, not the least bit interested in anything you have to offer. For our purposes, we'll assume the fish you have found are hungry.

One of the best baits for tarpon is a live crab, hooked through the side (see Chapter 3). Next would be a large and lively baitfish, and finally a large shrimp. Keep your bait fresh, changing it when it shows signs of losing vigor. For the most part, tarpon will be found in the deeper holes and channels in the backcountry. Most tarpon fishing on the flats is sight fishing, although regulars who have become familiar with travel patterns of local tarpon can do well by setting up in a particular place at a particular time with live bait. Because you're unfamiliar with the area and with the local tarpon in any given area, you don't have that option, for the most part.

Tarpon are generally first sighted at the surface. You may glimpse the fish itself or simply see the roiled water where a tarpon has "rolled," the term applied when a tarpon comes to the surface for a quick gulp of air. If you are in a relatively small area—say a few acres of deep water—and see a number of tarpon rolling, you can try putting out a live bait, preferably a lively baitfish such as a finger mullet, or a crab, suspended a couple of feet beneath a float.

By far the most common method of catching tarpon in the skinny water is sighting a fish and presenting a lure to it. Be sure to cast far enough from the fish to avoid startling it. There's a fine balance between getting the lure close enough to intercept the fish so he can see it and getting so close the fish is spooked, and only through practice will you develop a successful cast.

Tarpon will take pretty much the same artificials as snook; topwater and swimming plugs, jigs, spoons and large flies. For specifics, check in Chapter 9.

There are certain times and places where even a rank beginner to tarpon fishing can find a modicum of success. For example, tarpon follow huge schools of mullet that migrate down the east coast during summer, making frequent forays into the schools for a meal. With a boat, you can trail these schools, working the edges, with a good chance of a hookup. On the west coast, tarpon congregate in the deep passes during the summer, and can be taken on live white bait or jigs, and in the late spring small schools of tar-

Figure 8-5. This 73-year-old retired urologist had never caught a tarpon, but between 9 and 11 one morning, fishing with a guide, he brought three to the boat, each over 100 lbs.

pon can be seen making their way just off the beaches of the gulf, especially around the Charlotte Harbor/Sarasota area.

Working those gulf fish (known as the Manasota Mob for their abundance off Manasota Key near Boca Grande) is tricky fishing, as you must sight the fish and get yourself in a position where they will intercept you, not the other way around. You cannot sneak up on these fish, as you're sure to spook them. The proven method is to sight a few tarpon, get ahead of them and use your electric motor to position your boat in their line of travel, casting a live crab or baitfish to the edge of the school as they "daisy chain," swimming in a tight circle, head to tail.

Tarpon are also taken around bridges, most often at night, and usually with live bait. Landing a tarpon of decent size from a bridge is next to impossible without a bridge gaff, but then you run the risk of damaging the fish, and you have the problem of how to get it back into the water. *Remember, tarpon can only be*

Figure 8-6a. Tarpon circling head-to-tail at the surface, a peculiarity known as a "daisy chain." Flip a live crab or artificial bait ahead of a fish, on the outside of the circle, and . . .

Figure 8-6b. . . . moments later, you're hooked up with a hundred pounds or so of tarpon.

kept if you have purchased a tarpon tag, unless you're with a guide who has one, so not releasing it isn't an option in most cases. If you want to catch tarpon around a bridge, do it from a boat where you can easily release the fish.

In those parts of the state where tarpon are more or less permanent residents, small tarpon can be found in canals, bays, and boat basins with at least 6 feet of water and access to deeper water such as a river or the ICW. On the east coast, mosquito control canals on Hutchinson Island offer some fine fishing for small tarpon as well as the occasional redfish, snook, and trout. Inconsiderate anglers and hikers cause periodic damage, so check with the St. Lucie County Mosquito Control District first, to see if access is still being allowed.

I stand by my opening statement. The best way to ensure success with tarpon is to hire a guide. See Appendix 1 if you don't already have a guide in mind, preferably one with whom you or a friend have had successful trips. You'll learn enough in a trip or two to at least get you on the road toward self-sufficiency in tarpon hunting.

Trout

There are three types of saltwater trout found in Florida, all members of the drum family, which makes them cousins to the redfish. The sand seatrout, a small fish of generally less than a pound (the all-tackle IGFA record, set at Gulf Breeze on the Panhandle in November of 1994 by Matthew Finelli is one ounce over a pound), is found in the Gulf, although some are found in the Atlantic in the extreme southerly portions of the state. A pale body, yellow on the back shading to white below, the absence of well-defined spots and a yellow mouth are clues to identification.

Silver seatrout, the smallest of the Florida saltwater trout, are found on both coasts. A straw-colored back, silver sides, and white belly as well as the unique tail that is longer on the bottom than the top set this fish apart from a close relative, the silver perch. The clincher is the one or two prominent canine teeth, which the perch lack.

Finally, there is the spotted seatrout, the only one of the three found throughout the entire state, and the one to which most Floridians are referring when they say "trout." Smaller on the Gulf side (5 pounds would be rare), these trout routinely exceed 10 pounds on the east coast, where the current Florida record fish of more than 15 pounds was taken.

The family tree is about the only thing they have in common with redfish. Much smaller, trout feed primarily on shrimp and small fish. Don't try to land a trout by placing your thumb in its mouth; their canine teeth will easily inflict a serious and painful puncture. As their mouths are somewhat tender, lifting a trout into the boat with your rod is likely to result in losing the fish. A net is the best way to land trout of any kind or size without damaging the fish or having it tear off the hook.

Trout prefer grass beds and sandy or muddy bottoms. They don't move around much, so if you find them in a particular grassy area once, chances are they'll be there frequently. While redfish feed best on a dropping tide and snook when it's rising, trout care less about the direction in which the water's moving than the fact that it is moving. The first two hours of tidal flow, either in or out, are best for trout.

An overcast day will frequently bring trout to the surface, as does darkness. Large trout are often loners or at best travel with a very few others, almost always the same size class. Says Captain Greenan, "Often this means that the biggest ones are on oysters or other structures on the flood." (By "flood," Greenan means the very top of the incoming tide, just before it stops coming in.) "The young flood," he continues, "keeps them on the flat because of the abundance of food. Their larger prey will be exposed at the structure on the top half of the tide." You may find small groups or doubles in a given locale at a particular tidal stage.

If there's enough water at low tide, trout won't even leave a grass flat, they'll simply move to its deeper parts. They can be caught up against the mangroves, but rarely spend time up in the roots, preferring to hang out around the branches that hang over the water.

Figure 8-7. Larger trout will hit big topwater plugs such as this Zara Spook, but for most it would be more effective to use a Baby Zara or a propeller plug, such as a Dyin' Flutter.

Best bait is shrimp, and most people prefer live shrimp. While shrimp used for trout needn't be as large as those for snook or tarpon, they should be 3 to 4 inches long. A #1 hook is as large as you will need, and smaller hooks, down to about a number 4 will work. Pigfish, pinfish, grunts, and other white bait also work very well for trout. Grunts, especially, make a noise that attracts trout, and most trout caught that exceed 10 pounds are taken on live baitfish. You may have to use a slightly larger hook with large baitfish, but big trout (referred to as " 'gators") have a large enough mouth, and if you're using baitfish that large, 'gator trout are what you'll most likely attract.

A popping cork is very effective for trout, probably more than for any other species. Experiment with levels, moving the cork to fish your shrimp at various depths from the surface. This can be of great importance. I once watched as one bridge angler pulled in one trout after another while another angler, fishing 20 or 25 feet away couldn't buy a hit. I suggested he try different depths and he immediately began to catch trout.

Swimming plugs and jigs are the preferred lures for trout, although large trout will readily hit a surface lure. Experiment with different retrieves. One very popular and effective retrieve is to lift the rod tip high in a sweep of several feet, then lower the rod allowing the jig to fall back through the water. Hits will most likely come as the jig falls back. A variation is to lift the tip just as high, but to do it in a fast series of jerks. Again, the hit will probably come on a slack line. Finally, the jig can be retrieved relatively fast, with the rod tip down so the jig skims across the top of the grass.

Saltwater MirrOlures, especially the 52M and TT models, have probably accounted for more seatrout since their introduction in the early '50s than any other swimming plug. It's so popular and so effective that you'll probably be unable to find a place that doesn't stock some. Find a drug store that has one pegboard of fishing tackle for sale and MirrOlures will be on it. Not to say other swimming plugs don't work well. There are many productive lures, and more seem to come out every month. The Bill Lewis line, particularly the Rat-L-Trap, is very effective, and I especially like the relatively new floating model.

Best colors for trout are combinations of red and white, but the green-and-gold model is also a good producer. I favor red-and-white, and a few black spots are a nice addition.

Trout will readily take streamer flies in any of the patterns that imitate shrimp or small baitfish. The Bent Back Shrimp, tied by Dana Griffin, is one of my favorites. If the trout are in deeper water, weighted flies like the Clouser Minnow, Captain Greenan's Butthead, or a Seaducer with non-lead eyes, work best.

Whiting

While whiting are occasionally taken on jigs, by far the most effective means of catching them is with bait. Whiting hang out in the surf, surprisingly close to shore, so even beginners can cast far enough for them. Catching whiting is great fun for youngsters, as it requires little in the way of tackle. Because sand fleas are the preferred enticement, catching the bait can be almost as entertaining for them as catching the fish. A sand flea rake is recommended (see Chapter 3), but when the little "bugs" are plentiful a sufficient supply can usually be scooped up by hand.

A great second choice bait for whiting is . . . a piece of whiting. If sand fleas are proving uncooperative and a bit hard to find, filet the first whiting you catch and cut small pieces from the filets. It works surprisingly well.

Multiple hook rigs are common, but not really necessary. It's one of the things that make fishing for whiting so simple. A piece of bait on a single #1 or #2 hook fished above a small sinker using a light spinning rod to cast the bait thirty or forty feet from the shore at the beach is all that's needed.

Whiting are also quite tasty, and make an excellent choice for a seafood salad. Simply steam the fish until the flesh flakes away from the bones and skin, separate it, mix in your favorite salad dressing or some mayonnaise, chill and enjoy. For a special treat, add a small amount of crab meat to your mix and you'll swear it's all crab meat.

So there you have most of the more common and more popular species generally found in Florida's inshore waters. Also found in one place or another are bonefish, crawfish, croakers, groupers, permit and various shellfish. Most have been excluded because of restricted range, and crawfish and shellfish are covered in Chapter 12. Go catch some, and have fun.

Chapter 9

Using Artificials— Which Ones and How

There's always a certain amount of risk in recommending artificial lures, for any type of fishing. First, there's the matter of personal choice and confidence. The latter plays a big part in the success of a given lure, as an angler without confidence in the lure is likely to be more casual about its use than about one that has done well in the past. In addition, a lure not yet on the market may well supplant today's big producer, and no writer of the outdoors wants to mislead readers by appearing to ignore a lure when the fact is the writer, no more clairvoyant than the reader, simply had no knowledge of its development.

I catch 90% of my fish on three or four lures, simply because I use them more often than others. Nearly all the fish I catch on topwater plugs, for example, are taken on either a Zara Spook or a Pop-R. Does this mean the Rebel Jumpin' Minnow is not as effective as the Zara, even though it has a similar action? Of course not, and if I used the Jumpin' Minnow as often as I use the Zara, I'd catch more fish on it.

The important point is that if you have a favorite lure that's always produced well for you, don't assume it won't work because it isn't "made for Florida." Let's take a look at lure types first, then we'll get into specifics, such as models and colors.

First, however, there's one very important caveat that just can't be over emphasized, and that is the need for quality hooks intended for use in saltwater. Hooks meant for freshwater simply will not stand up in the briny, and I don't mean they'll only last a month or two. It's more like one trip before rust and corrosion set in. Ignoring the rust factor, many Florida saltwater fish, such as jacks, redfish, and snook, will straighten or snap some of the light hooks used for freshwater fish. If you want to use a favorite lure that doesn't have saltwater hooks on it, buy some and change them out.

Color in General

I'll address the issue of color separately, because most of the theory applies equally to all lure types. Conventional wisdom says that you use bright lures under poor visibility conditions, dark colors when visibility is good. The theory holds that when it's difficult for a fish to see your lure you make it easier, while the fish needs no help when it can see well. Up to a point, that's quite true, but like so many other things, it can be carried too far.

Keep in mind the reason you're selecting a color in the first place. You are, or should be, selecting one that will appear to be that of your quarry's natural food. Not an exact match, but something that at least resembles the food eaten by the fish you're after. Browns and tans, for example, to imitate crabs and other crustaceans, white combined with other colors to resemble baitfish.

Those natural foods are in the same place you're fishing; that's why you're fishing there. If the water is murky from mud and sediment, or stained by tannin from trees or peat, you might want to help the fish see your lure by using a light color. By the same reasoning, you can use more subdued colors in clear water.

But the name of the game with artificials is "natural," and it isn't natural for one baitfish or crab to stand out enormously from those around it. In the wild, be it fish or game, "unusual" generally means danger, and if you overdo the visibility angle you may actually scare fish off. You don't want your lure to be a paint horse grazing in a herd of zebras.

If the degree of visibility is due not to murky or clean water, but to ambient light conditions, it's more important than ever to try to use colors that will appear natural. Dark colors present a better, more visible silhouette, and should be used during early morning and late evening hours, when a silhouette is all the fish can see to begin with. On cloudy days (yes, we do get them in Florida) there will frequently be good light but no brightness. The sky is completely covered, as opposed to a normal bright day with a clear and bright blue sky. These overcast days are good days to try your topwater lures.

The whole matter can be stated as a simple rule of thumb for jigs, plugs, and flies: Dark days, dark colors; bright days, bright colors; overcast days, stay on top.

As with most rules having to do with fishing, this one is more a guideline than a hard-and-fast principle, and there will be exceptions. Start out by following the guideline for colors, but don't get locked into it. If what you're using isn't working, try a color that's "wrong." I won't tell, honest. Finally, as Lefty Kreh pointed out in his excellent book *Fly Fishing in Salt Water,* ". . . everywhere you fish you will find some baitfish that have a dark green or blue back and silvery sides and belly." Your selection of both swimming plugs and flies should include something in this pattern.

Jigs

There's an age-old discussion that makes the rounds of fishing clubs regularly, and was probably kicked around in front of wood stoves in fishing camps generations ago, and that is "What one lure would you want if you were stranded on a remote island with no food?"

For my money, it would have to be a jig. In an appropriate color and worked properly, jigs can be made to imitate crabs, small fish, shrimp, or squid. A jig is as close to a universal lure as anything you'll ever find in a tackle shop, and it will take fish in any waters under various conditions. Nothing is perfect, and there will be times when a jig just won't produce, but given a situation under which fish will hit an artificial lure, you'll find a jig has the least chance of being ignored of any type.

Types of Jigs

While there are several basic types of jig heads available today, round (also called ball) or oval (bullet) heads seem to produce best. Flat (coin) jigs can be very useful when fishing for such bottom-hugging species as flounder; and a disk jig, looking like a flat jig turned on its side, can really get to the bottom quickly in deep water. Slant jigs (the head is cut on an angle) are great for imitating the quick, darting movement of a small baitfish.

All this notwithstanding, ball jigs such as the Trout Tout that gave plastic-tailed jigs their start in Florida back in the '50s, or oval jigs, such as the Cotee Liv'Eye, are most common and are extremely effective. (See Figure 9-1.) Jigs with nylon, feathers, or deer hair (bucktail) also work well, but come with two built-in

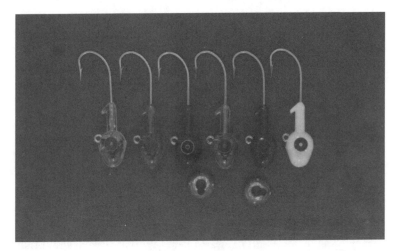

Figure 9-1. The Cotee Liv'Eye jig has a hollow plastic head filled with a "rattle material," and comes with a ring that can be slipped on to change the weight from ⅛ to ¼ ounce.

disadvantages. First, you can't easily change the color, and second, the many sharp-toothed fish found in Florida will make pretty short work of tails in these materials.

Marabou, as an example, is an excellent jig tail material. It dyes easily and has a unique floating, breathing action that is particularly lifelike. However, marabou feathers, taken from under the wing of the stork of the same name, are extremely delicate and fragile, and catching just a few fish on one will have it looking like an emaciated bison shedding its winter coat. If you like to tie your own jig dressing, try marabou. When you can replace the tail materials yourself, the cost is relatively low, and the action can't be matched by any other material I know of.

Bucktail and nylon jigs have a very definite place in Florida fishing, because of their relative durability. While feather and plastic tails are effective with bluefish, nothing will outlast nylon against their teeth.

The amazing variety of shapes and colors available in plastic tails can be quite bewildering, especially for those who feel they need every new gadget to come along. The fact is just a few simple shapes in a variety of colors is all you need. A tackle box can accommodate only a given number of tails, so it's better to concentrate on a variety of colors than to try to have five tails in every shape available.

Shapes and Colors of Jigs

Besides all that, basic shapes can be easily altered. Figure 9-2 shows just three methods of cutting the flat portion of a plastic grub tail to change the way it appears in the water, a technique shared by pro guide Roger Johnson of Inverness, Florida. While the results of the cone and split tail modifications are easily imagined, the effect of the third method is not so obvious.

Slicing in a slightly curved arc from the edge at the base of the flat tail to a point approximately three-fourths of the way to the tip will cause the grub to act like a curly tail, with a rapid, fluttering swimming motion. It's just a cut; don't remove material. You can probably come up with a few modifications of your own;

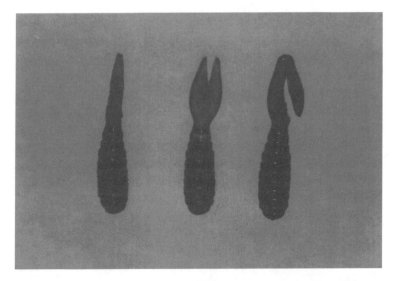

Figure 9-2. Three ways to alter the shape of a plastic tail to change its action. Slicing it in a arc, as on the far right, converts it to the equivalent of a curly tail.

experimentation by anglers has probably led to more lure shapes and modifications than have the trials of factory engineers.

Red or maroon heads are generally effective, but you should also include white and yellow. With a wide variety of plastic tail colors in your box, you should be able to find the right combination in relatively short order. Following the rule of thumb previously discussed will help reduce the number of attempts you have to make in your selections. Color names vary from manufacturer to manufacturer, but something resembling the color of root beer should be one of the tail colors in your box, as should white, a translucent off-white, chartreuse, red, pink, purple, and yellow or gold.

Don't hesitate to experiment with colors, even if the combination seem unlikely. I once half-jokingly flipped a yellow plastic worm with black polka dots against a bank of the St. Lucie River and a fish nailed it on the first cast. My son and I spent the next half-hour speculating on just what the fish could possibly thought he was about to eat. If the fish aren't hitting what you're offering, give them a choice.

White tails with a bright red or orange tip are quite effective, but it's likely pigfish, pinfish, and other small denizens of the grass flats will bite the tips off quickly. Some of these baitfish are quite aggressive, and if the sailor's choice grew to 20 pounds, I'd be afraid to toss out a Zara for fear one would take it away from me. I've caught 6-inch sailor's choice on plugs longer than the fish.

Working the Jig

The manner in which you'll work a jig will vary according to what you're trying to catch. If you're working a grass bed for trout, retrieve the jig with a darting action to imitate a small baitfish, or alternately lift and lower the rod tip in a long sweep as you reel to make the jig look like a shrimp. Lift the rod tip without reeling, and reel in the slack line as you allow the jig to fall back. Most of your hits will come as the jig falls. You can use this same motion to hop the jig across the bottom of sandy holes in the grass flats, except with a greatly reduced sweep. Don't forget to work the grass edges around the holes. That's where reds, snook, and trout will be lurking. Flounders are more likely to stay on the mud or sand.

Working along the mangroves and edges for snook or redfish, where the water is too shallow for the long, sweeping rod tip action, hop the jig along the bottom or use shorter strokes of the rod to keep the jig moving in that darting baitfish manner.

For flounders over muddy or sandy bottom or short grass, slow the retrieve down to keep the jig near the bottom, and use short, swift jerks to give it action.

Jigging for pompano is generally done from a bridge, pier, or boat. Let the jig go all the way to the bottom, then take a few turns of the reel handle and commence jigging, moving the rod tip a foot or two, then letting the jig fall back. Again, the hits will generally come on the drop. Vary the depth until you find the level at which the fish are moving. It's most likely within a few feet of the bottom, as pompano feed primarily on crabs and sand fleas. Yellow or white-and-yellow jigs are best for pompano. In some areas, a simple can pole is used.

For bluefish, jacks, and ladyfish, just make the jig move. If something is moving, these fish figure it must be edible.

Tandem rigs—one jig trailing another—work quite well, especially for trout. If you prefer not to make up your own, Love's Lures of St. Petersburg offers an excellent selection of ready-made tandem rigs in various size and color combinations.

We all develop our favorites in lures, and where jigs are concerned, mine is the Cotee Liv'Eye. In several sizes, with and without a weed guard, the Cotee jigs have super sharp saltwater hooks. It's a tough "typical" jig to beat, in my experience. The Rattlin' Liv'Eye offers the added advantages of noise and of a collar that can be slipped on to increase the weight. You can add the collar to fish channels and deep holes, then simply slip it off if you want to move to the shallower waters over a grass bed. The hollow plastic head is filled with "shot" and gives off a distinct sound as the jig is worked.

One of the features that endears the Cotee rattling jig to me is the eye that gives the Liv'Eye line its name. Large eyes on lures and jigs have been known for many years to attract fish, and the eye on the Cotee jig stands out a long way off. Looking for all the world like a stick-on decal, the eye is actually welded by a sonic method that ensures it won't come off.

Another great line of jigs comes from D.O.A. Fishing Lures of Palm City, Florida. These lures are soft plastic molded into extremely lifelike models of baitfish, crabs, and shrimp, with a good, strong saltwater hook embedded. They can be worked in the same manner as an ordinary jig, of course, but unlike ordinary jigs, they can also be live-lined (See Chapter 4).

Enhancers

No discussion of jigs would be complete without a few words about enhancers, sometimes incorrectly called attractants. An attractant is something that causes a fish to find your lure, such as chum or products manufactured for that specific purpose. An enhancer is something added to a lure to increase the likelihood that a fish, having found your lure, will try to eat it. Using an enhancer, you must still get the fish close enough through good casting and skillful manipulation of the lure. Attractants can be thought of as dinner bells; enhancers are the gravy.

There are several such substances on the market, but the enhancer with which I've had the most success is ProBait from Cotee Bait Company. The product, developed after 10 years of research at the University of Florida's Whitney Marine Research Laboratory, comes in two sizes, Tip-it and the larger Chunk-it. ProBait consists of a material biochemically similar to natural baits such as shrimp, bonded to a strong mesh material, and will last for a couple of dozen casts before it begins to lose its ability to give off scent. Available in shrimp and other "flavors," ProBait is inexpensive and requires no refrigeration or other special care.

A number of plastic worm manufacturers have come out with lures impregnated with various scents, all of which work in the same way as ProBait, with the advantage of not being an "add-on," and there are liquids that can be put on plugs without changing the lure's action. Some of these are actual attractants, such as Riverside's "Real Baitfish," advertised as "A school of baitfish in every bottle." Kodiak Scent Company has scents in various forms; oils, paste, powder and a soak solution. Unlike many others, part of their line specifically targets saltwater fish, using scents of their natural foods; anchovy, ballyhoo (balao), herring, mullet, shrimp, and squid.

I don't use ProBait or other enhancers all the time, but they are quite effective on those days when fish will follow your jig with obvious interest, but just don't want to pick it up. Using an enhancer will quite frequently add that extra touch needed for a hookup.

Swimming Plugs

It would seem obvious there's no call for deep-diving swimming plugs in inshore Florida, and that would be true were it not for bridges, piers, and deeper parts of the ICW, inlets, and passes. Be sure to have a few diving plugs with you, especially fishing at night. While snook love to hang out near the lights and can frequently be seen right near the surface, they are sometimes ten or more feet below the surface. Various models of Bomber, Creek Chub, Heddon, MirrOlure, Rapala, and Rebel diving plugs have all worked for me, although if pressed for a choice, I'd have to single out the MirrOlure TT series as my favorite when snook are deep, with the Rebel Minnow a close second.

Figure 9-3. One of the most popular lures in Florida since its introduction in 1944, the MirrOlure continues to catch fish consistently. Shown here is the TT28, popular for redfish and trout.

I'm sure you have your own favorites, so give them a try, just remember the earlier warning about hooks. Many of the fish you'll find in these deeper waters are quite large, especially the snook. In the same vein, you'll need a stiff rod and at least 20- or even 30-pound-test line.

All that notwithstanding, most of the swimming plugs you'll use will be shallow runners, because most of your fishing will probably be up in the backcountry and other skinny water areas, where the fish are found in six feet or less of water.

Here you'll want such lures as MirrOlures in the 52M series, the Smithwick RA or RB Rattlin' Rogue, the Cordell C85 Ripplin' Red Fin, or one of the Heddon Minnows. A swimming plug that's fast becoming a favorite of mine over the grass beds is the saltwater model of the floating Rat-L-Trap from Bill Lewis Lures. Most of the trout I've caught on swimming plugs in the past thirty years have been taken on a MirrOlure 52M26, although I've lately been having good success with the S39MR. The "S" indicates the lure has a single hook instead of the usual treble hooks.

I've long felt the array of hooks found on today's plugs is often overkill, and detracts from casting distance in the bargain, and the S39 confirmed that for me. It's the same size as the 39MR series, yet the extra distance on a cast has to be seen to be believed. While it's true that accuracy is more important in the skinny water than distance, it's nice when blind casting grass beds for trout to be able to cover more water per cast. As far as I can determine, there has been negligible difference in the percentage of hookups on hits with only one hook.

I prefer swimming plugs that float over those that sink, as it allows you to let the plug drift to the surface, then dive it down toward the grass as though it were an injured baitfish trying for the sanctity of a hiding place. Along those lines, the new suspending baits should do quite well under the same conditions, and the Storm SuspenDot system appears to me to be something with definite potential for trout and redfish in particular.

SuspenDots (actually, there are both dots and strips) are small decals with an adhesive backing that can be placed on a lure to alter its buoyancy, thus the level at which a suspending bait will suspend. A floating bait can also be made into a floater/diver, diving twitch baits can be made to dive deeper or faster, and so on. As a bonus, they can also add a few yards to a cast, but as we've seen, that isn't a critical factor in the skinny water.

The dots are three-eighths of an inch around, and the strips measure one-quarter inch by one inch. They can be cut or placed one on top of the other to increase or decrease the amount of weight they add to a lure. It sure beats trying to wrap something around a hook to add weight, or drilling holes to insert metal pieces or shot. One disadvantage to the latter method is that it's a permanent change, whereas SuspenDots are easily placed and removed.

On the flats, use swimming plugs over grass beds and in the channels on and between the flats. Basically, you can use a swimming plug anywhere you can use a jig, with the obvious exception of water so shallow the plug hits bottom and hangs up. By far the most productive use of swimming plugs in the skinny water is over grass beds and on grass flats. Vary your retrieve all the way from a fast, steady swimming action to a slower jerky retrieve until you hit on the action fish will find attractive on any given day.

Although trout are what you're most likely to find on grass beds, redfish, snook, tarpon, and the occasional cobia will all take swimming plugs within their respective ranges. Jack crevalle, ladyfish, Spanish mackerel, and, especially during the winter, bluefish are common on the grass beds and flats, and all will readily attack a swimming plug. Most of these species hit with good authority.

Combinations of red and white, yellow and white, green and white and green and gold are generally best. Chartreuse is a great daytime color, especially on bright days, and little tricks such as using a trailer, either a small jig or a tiny plug such as the ultra-light MirrOlures will frequently turn up fish on very slow days. Swimming plugs can also be used as trailers behind topwater baits, especially popping plugs.

Topwater Plugs

By far my favorite way to catch skinny water fish, topwater plugs can be quite effective when used properly. While many anglers grab for a topwater plug any time the surface is dead calm, the fact is they work best when the water is a bit agitated. I don't mean whitecaps, but just a bit of a wind ripple on top.

The Zara Spook, Jumpin' Minnow, and similar plugs are quite productive, but it takes a bit of practice to learn the proper retrieve. If you already know how to "walk the dog," fine, but for those who don't, here's how it's done. On the retrieve, the rod tip is whipped back in a short arc, more like a medium-fast jerk. The plug moves forward and to one side, due to the shape of the head, and stops when you give slack at the end of the jerk. On the next twitch, the plug moves again, but to the other side. This results in a side-to-side, flopping action, with just a hint of splash. You can pause from time to time, but most often walking the dog is a steady retrieve.

While not as good in plastic as it was when Stan Gibbs was making them out of wood, the Pencil Popper from Cordell is another plug that can be walked in this way, and it more closely resembles a needlefish or small ladyfish than do the others, so it's a good addition to any tackle box. If your time in Florida is limited, you may want to pass on these lures, unless you can practice before you get here, but at some time or another, you should learn this retrieve if you don't already know it, because it's effective in fresh water as well as salt, and Zara Spooks have accounted for many a largemouth bass.

Zaras, Jumpin' Minnows, Pencil Poppers, and some of the new stickbaits designed for this type of action will take snook, tarpon,

Figure 9-4. The Zara Spook family of topwater plugs, including two (bottom center, top left) that were experimental prototypes and are no longer available.

and 'gator trout, although most small trout will give them only a cursory look or hit tentatively. They are especially good for snook, which prefer a more subtle topwater bait than do many other gamefish. More than half the snook I've caught have been taken on Zara Spooks, with the rest unevenly divided between jigs and swimming plugs, in that order. I have one rod and reel combination that has never had any lure but various Zara Spooks on it. I keep it rigged and handy no matter where I'm fishing, just in case.

Popping plugs also work well on the flats. The Pop-R (Rebel), Chugger Spook (Heddon), and Spitfire (Bill Lewis Lures) are good examples of effective popping plugs. For trout, a good pop with plenty of splash is most successful, but for snook you'll need to tone it down a bit, which is probably a major reason the Mirr-Olure Surface Popper, with its small popping surface catches so many more snook than trout.

For snook, shorter twitches of the rod will suffice. Maybe it's a sign they're better predators, but you don't have to whack the surface of the water with a board to suggest to a snook there's an injured fish struggling there. Trout seem to need all the help they can get.

While redfish will try to grab an easy surface meal as quickly as any other predator, the placement and size of their mouth makes it difficult for them to really nail a surface plug, although they will do so often enough to make it worth trying. Recently, I've been having good redfish success with the Spitfire.

Injured Minnow lures such as the Heddon Dying Flutter, the Devil's Horse from Smithwick and MirrOlure's Surface Spinner are super baits for trout, especially over the grass beds. Make a big splash by twitching the rod, then let the plug settle for a bit, then twitch and reel again. There are times when a steady, pumping retrieve work well for trout, and you should in any case vary the speed of retrieve from time to time. Injured minnow type lures and those like the Zara are excellent producers at first light and just before dark. Use darker colors, even black. One thing is certain, and that's the way fish in shallow Florida waters attack surface plugs; with a vengeance. All that commotion seems to bring out the worst in them. Be prepared for some smashing strikes.

Spoons

We started at the bottom, came up to the top, and now we're going back down again to look at another effective lure, the spoon. Spoons will take most of the fish in the skinny water, and in that sense it's a universal lure, similar to jigs in range of use and the species that will take it. Gold is probably best, but silver spoons will also work, and some in fact prefer them. Personally, I favor a gold Johnson spoon, but the Cotee Liv'Eye spoon is also quite effective.

Spoons are the lure of choice for many anglers who target redfish on the flats, and just about the best choice if you think cobia are in the area. They're good when sight fishing, enabling accurate casts within the range usually available to sight casters. It's best to cast beyond your target and let the fish intercept the lure. Blind casting with a spoon over grass beds will produce not only redfish and cobia, but some nice trout.

Now, a lure for which you are probably unprepared, just as I was when I first tried it. The incredibly unlikely Solo lure, as

Figure 9-5. Spoons are very effective inshore, taking cobia, reds, snook, and trout. Here is a ¼-oz Cotee; it's also available in a ½-oz size.

Figure 9-6. This unlikely-looking but very effective Solo lure, as weedless as any lure can be, can be worked through mangrove roots for snook or crawled over oysters for redfish.

close to totally weedless as any lure can be, was originally developed for largemouth bass, but when a representative handed me one and said "Try it, you'll like it," all I could see in my mind were oyster bars and grass flats.

Essentially a hollow, cone-shaped piece of soft plastic with a skirt and a treble hook, the Solo can be swum across the surface or, with the addition of a small egg sinker, walked right on the bottom. A leader is threaded through a hole at the pointed end of the cone, the sinker added or omitted depending on how the lure is to be used, and then the leader is tied to the treble hook. (See Figure 9-6.)

At the bottom of the fat end of the cone is an indented area into which the points of the treble hook are placed. This effectively shields the hooks and prevents them from snagging on anything—and I do mean anything. About the only way you can hang up this lure is to cast over a branch in such a way that the lure revolves around the branch, winding your line around it, or if the treble hook comes out of its protective pocket. Checking the lure every once in a while prevents the latter. When a fish picks up the lure, the soft plastic is squeezed in and the hook points exposed.

The Solo can be walked or bounced right across oyster bars and through dense marine grasses, just the places where redfish are looking for a meal, and casting the mangroves for snook becomes much less risky in terms of hangups. With less weight added you can swim it right across the top of grass beds, or you can remove

all weight and work it on top. I'm not suggesting you replace all
your lures with a Solo, merely saying that it's a handy lure to have
for those places you want to try but haven't been able to for fear
of hanging up and losing a lure.

Flies

While the glamour species such as bonefish, permit, and tarpon
get most of the press aimed at fly casters, nearly every species of
fish found in the skinny water can and probably has been caught
on flies. Possible exceptions are selective feeders such as
sheepshead, but I wouldn't bet against that, either.

By far the most effective flies used in inshore Florida waters are
streamers, but that's where the limitations end. You'll find color
selection and combinations debated by skinny water fly fishermen
as enthusiastically as at any salmon or freshwater fishing club.

Phil Chapman, a fish research biologist with the Florida Fish &
Game Commission, is an outstanding fly fisherman who spends
as many of his recreational hours as he can on the water. He and
his wife, Debbie, also an excellent fly tackle angler, primarily
prowl the backcountry and the flats for tarpon, but don't pass up
any opportunity to catch other species. I asked Phil what fly selection advice he would offer an angler unfamiliar with inshore
Florida fly fishing.

"If a person isn't familiar with which particular color or pattern
produces consistently for a given species in a given area," said
Chapman, "my suggestion for an all-around fly would be a
Clouser Minnow. I'd stay with the natural colors, for example,
white to imitate fish and brown for crustaceans, as opposed to the
brighter colors less commonly found in nature such as floures-
cents, reds, etc. If you aren't sure about size," he added, "err on
the side of too small rather than too large."

Up until a few years ago, most of those who specialize in fly
fishing the flats and backcountry would have agreed the one fly
they wouldn't be without was a Lefty's Deceiver. Today, most
would agree with Chapman that the Clauser Minnow is also an
excellent choice for an all-around inshore fly, effective on all the

major gamefish from flounder to tarpon.

Here are some other favorites from a couple of experts, one on each coast, both professional guides who fish inshore Florida. Captain Greenan fishes primarily on the southwest coast in the general area of Charlotte Harbor and Captain Kumiski the east coast.

Redfish

Greenan's first choice would be his own Greenan Redfish Fly, followed by a popper in red and white, a Clauser Minnow in chartreuse, black or gray, a brown and olive crab fly, and a tan shrimp fly, all tied on #1 hooks.

Kumiski's choices are a Clauser Minnow, a Fuzzy Crab and a Seaducer.

Snook

Greenan picks a Finger Mullet pattern in red-and-white, then a Greenback Finger Mullet, a Greenback Deceiver, either a chartreuse-and-white Deceiver (yellow in water stained by tannin), a Clauser, and for fishing around lights at night a pearl Glass Minnow.

Kumiski picks large Deceivers, a Rattlin' Minnow, and says it's a coin toss for third choice between a large hair bug and a Seaducer.

Tarpon

Greenan likes a Black Death, Cockroach, and an orange and grizzly combination in the morning, a blue with grizzly and gold anytime during the day, a chartreuse and yellow, and a purple and black combination for the backcountry. The chartreuse/yellow and the purple/black are tied on a 1/O hook, the others on a 4/O.

Kumiski says a Cockroach, anything with grizzly and something orange and brown.

Personal Fly Favorites

Notice how often the Clauser shows up on the lists from these experts. While there may well be better choices for a specific area and species, you won't go wrong with a Clauser Minnow or a Lefty's Deceiver, no matter where you are in Florida's inshore waters, and no matter the species. Here are a few more choices from my own fly box.

For trout, I like Greenan's Butthead in purple-and-black, a Clauser Minnow or a Bend-Back Shrimp.

For redfish, the Bend Back Crab, the Greenan Redfish Fly or a Clauser.

When it comes to snook I'll go with Greenan's choices, but add a large yellow-and-white streamer and, especially for smaller snook, a popping bug. For tarpon, a Cockroach or a Deceiver.

The Bend Back Shrimp and Bend Back Crab are available from Dana Griffin, of Gainesville, Florida, otherwise known as the Florida Fly Tyer. Griffin has several special patterns and his mail-order prices are quite reasonable. If you plan to do much fly fishing in Florida, his is a catalog you'll want to have. Another good source is Captain James Wood, a fishing guide based in Terra Ceia on Florida's west coast. (See Appendix 1 for addresses.)

As with other artificial lures, jacks and ladyfish will hit just about any fly you toss their way. A fast retrieve will usually generate more strikes from these two. For bluefish and mackerel use streamers with mylar strips or other reflective material for flash. Don't forget about their teeth, and check your leader frequently.

Fishing the backcountry, a weed guard is helpful, especially around the mangroves. Try to include in your fly box patterns that have an eye painted white with a black pupil and some red near the head to represent gills. The red must be visible when viewed from the gamefish's attack angle.

Chapter 10

Limits, Seasons, Rules, and Regulations

Saltwater regulations are in a more or less constant state of flux in Florida. For that reason, do not take the following as current. Chances are there have been changes, and you should avail yourself of publications that contain up-to-date information. Most places that sell saltwater fishing licenses will have them, or you can call or write either the Florida Marine Patrol or the Florida Department of Environmental Protection (DEP). (See Appendix 1.)

The following, then, should be taken only as a guide, as a list of things that are regulated, and the types of limits you're likely to encounter. Note that not only fish are regulated, and that some species require a special stamp in addition to a saltwater license. If you're fishing with a professional guide, you won't need any of them.

Only species that are likely to be encountered inshore on a regular basis are included here, no billfish or other offshore species.

Licenses and Stamps

First, there is the matter of a license. Florida has separate licenses for fresh and saltwater fishing. You will need one unless you are—

1. Under the age of 16, or a Florida resident over the age of 65.
2. A Florida resident fishing in saltwater from land (you can wade out to a depth of 4 feet) or from a structure fixed to land (this does not apply to piers unless the pier has a valid Pier Saltwater Fishing License).
3. Fishing from a boat that has a valid Vessel Saltwater Fishing License (this is why no license or stamps are needed when fishing with a professional guide—he or she has already bought a Vessel License, and half the tarpon tag allotment is reserved for guides).
4. A Florida resident fishing for mullet in freshwater and have a valid Florida Freshwater License.
5. A Florida resident fishing for a saltwater species in freshwater from land or from a structure fixed to the land.
6. A commercial fishermen, member of the Armed Forces under certain circumstances, or participant in certain Department of Health and Rehabilitation programs.

If you are a Florida resident and are certified as totally and permanently disabled, you can get a permanent license from your county tax collector.

In order to take crawfish or snook, a special stamp for that species must be purchased in addition to the license. A tag is required if a tarpon is to be kept.

Rules

The following rules are edited and summarized from the book *Fishing Lines,* available from the Florida DEP, and do not contain the full text. "Multiple hook" refers to such things as treble hooks.

Bay Scallops: No mechanical harvesting gear in water less than 3 feet deep. There are further restrictions by date and in certain areas.

Crabs, blue: You must have a special permit from the DEP to use more than five traps, and must work traps during daylight hours only.

Crabs, Stone: Must be released alive; only the claw can be taken, but not from egg-bearing females. Trapping requires a permit from the DEP. No device that might crush, puncture, or otherwise injure the crab's body may be used.

Crawfish (Spiny Lobster or Florida Lobster): Must remain in whole condition at all times while on or below Florida waters. No egg-bearing females may be taken. You cannot use grabs, grains (see Glossary), hooks or similar devices, and must have with you a device for measuring the carapace. Crawfish may not be taken within the Biscayne Bay Card Sound Sanctuary (in Dade and Monroe Counties) at any time. There is a special season during which only sportsmen (as opposed to commercial fishermen) can take crawfish, usually the last consecutive Wednesday and Thursday in July.

Black Drum: Multiple hooks cannot be used with live or dead natural bait. Snatching prohibited.

Hard Clams: You can't take or possess hard clams on the water from a half-hour after sunset through a half-hour before sunrise. There are specific regulations concerning the size and use of tongs.

Oysters: Can only be taken from areas specifically approved for the harvesting of shellfish, and only between sunrise and sunset. You can't use a drag, dredge, etc.

Pompano: Multiple hooks cannot be used with live or dead natural bait. Snatching prohibited.

Redfish: Hook-and-line only. You cannot use a multiple hook with live or dead bait.

Seatrout: Multiple hooks cannot be used with live or dead natural bait. Snatching prohibited.

Shrimp: A maximum of five gallons (heads on) per day per person, and one five-gallon bucket per day per boat. With a net registration, you can trawl with a net of 16 feet or less; larger nets require a Saltwater Products License.

Snook: Hook-and-line only. Multiple hooks (for example, a treble hook) cannot be used with live or dead natural bait. Snatching prohibited.

All marine animals, turtles, and turtle eggs and nests are protected species in Florida, and it's *never* legal to take a queen conch. Simply stay away from manatees, porpoises, turtles and such and you'll be certain of being on the right side of the law. Don't take a sample of the pretty coral home for your aquarium, either, as it's unlawful to destroy, possess, or take hard corals, fire corals, or sea fans.

Spearfishing regulations are complex and specific, and vary from area to area. Check with local authorities. The same applies to regulations concerning nets; contact the Marine Patrol.

Florida has a tough litter law, and in addition to ordinary litter, there is a specific regulation against discarding any monofilament line into or onto the water. Discarded line can be a killer. Save your old line until you get off the water, then take it to a Berkley dealer, who will gladly take it for recycling into plastic products (not new fishing line, but bottles, etc.).

Limits—Bag, Season, and Size

Some fish found in Florida's inshore waters have limits on when they can be taken, what size they must be, and how many can be kept. As earlier noted, if a tarpon is to be taken, a special tag must be purchased beforehand. The same caveat applies here as it did to the regulations previously listed; they are subject to change, and some may have already done so. Check with the Marine Patrol for the latest regulations and limits.

Possibly the most confusing of Florida's size limit laws are the "one-fish-exception" provisions. These apply to those species that have a "slot limit." This means a fish must fall within a minimum and a maximum length. A few examples may help to illustrate the manner in which the exceptions are applied. Again, and I can't emphasize this enough, there may have been changes.

Black Drum: .... Bag limit of 5 per day
Not less than 14″
Not more than 24″
Cannot possess more than one over 24″

Redfish:...................... Bag limit of 1 per day
                Not less than 18"
                Not more than 27"
                Closed season March, April, and May

Snook:...................... Bag limit of 2 per day
                Not less than 24"
                Not more than 34"
                Cannot possess more than one over 34"
                Closed season January, February, June,
                July, and August

Spotted Seatrout
Spotted Weakfish:........... Bag limit of 10 per day
                Not less than 14"
                Not more than 24"
                Cannot possess more than one over 24"

The significant point is that the regulations stipulate a "slot"—a range of maximum and minimum lengths. The rules say you cannot possess a redfish under 14" or over 24" in length. They say the same thing about black drum, snook, and trout. Then they say, "But not really."

There is a logic, however obscure it may appear at first, to this reasoning. In the case of black drum, snook, and trout, the rules allow you to keep more than one and state that of those one may exceed the maximum length. It allows an angler to keep one trophy fish while ensuring any other large fish will be returned. Because you can only keep one redfish per day, it obviously must meet the slot limit.

The purpose of a slot limit is to try to ensure that both juvenile fish and mature breeders will be returned to maintain the fisheries. Having only a minimum size might well result in too many spawning sized fish being taken from the waters, resulting inevitably in a reduction of young fish.

The success with restrictions on the taking of snook has encouraged closed seasons and prohibition of sale on other species, such as redfish. A strong resurgence in recent years in the number of redfish has proven that to have been a wise move, and it's likely that similar restrictions will be placed on such species as spotted seatrout, possibly even in place by the time you read this.

While they may seem a hodgepodge, there are justifications for the many regulations. Snook, for example, are a warm water fish, and cold spells—yes, we do get them in Florida—leave them sluggish and vulnerable to snagging, be it accidental or deliberate. The summer closure is, as with redfish, intended to protect the fishery during the months of spawning.

Bag and size limits, closed seasons, restrictions against sale of certain more popular species and the recent ban against most inshore netting are all intended to try to restore Florida's fisheries to the status they enjoyed back in the '40s and '50s. As great as the fishing is now, it's hard to believe it was once better, but it was, trust me, and we're hoping to restore it.

Catch and Release

One of the unfavorable side effects of these restrictions has been a new interest in catch-and-release by some who had never practiced it before. While catch-and-release is not in itself inherently bad—quite the contrary, it's good when practiced properly—a lack of experience and of knowledge of the proper procedures frequently results in the release of fish that are for all practical purposes dead, or so severely damaged they soon will be.

For those of you unfamiliar with catch-and-release, here are a few pointers.

Remove or flatten the barb on your hooks. Anglers have become so accustomed to reliance on the barb there's a feeling shared by many that a fish can't be landed without a large, sharp barb. Well, folks, when I take a new lure out of its box, the first thing I do is flatten the barbs on all the hooks, and I don't lose any more fish than the next guy. If a fish is properly hooked, with a hook of the appropriate size, and played correctly with a tight line, it won't get off any more easily than if the hook had a barb.

When I replace hooks on any of my plugs, I use a special hook from Mustad that is made without a barb. They come in all the sizes you'll need and are of high quality. If you'd like to explore this method, and I recommend it highly, see Appendix 1 for ordering information, including three shops in Florida that stock the hooks. (For the record, I have no connection with or financial interest in the Mustad company. I just like their products.)

Lack of a barb makes removing a fish a simple operation, and it frequently eliminates completely the need to even touch a fish or remove it from the water. Use of a tool especially designed for the purpose makes hook removal a simple operation. I personally favor the Dehooker, which comes in several sizes and takes about ten minutes of practice. (See Figure 10-1.) A package of Dehookers includes not only directions on using the tool, but also a few good tips on safely releasing fish. To use a Dehooker, you simply slide the end of the tool down the line or leader until it encounters the hook, give it a twist, and watch the fish swim off. The device could have been invented just for me, as I generally operate on the KISS principle—Keep It Simple, Stupid.

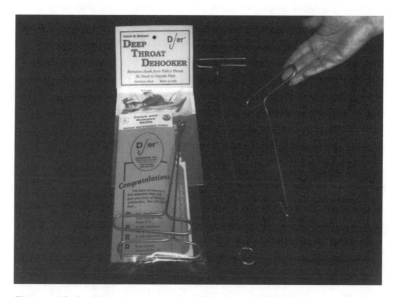

Figure 10-1. The Dehooker is a simple device that makes releasing a fish simple and safe. Most often, the fish need not even be removed from the water or handled in any way.

Don't play a fish to exhaustion unless you're absolutely certain you aren't going to put it back. (See Chapter 11 for information on lactic acid buildup.) This means you have identified the species, know with certainty it's of a legal size to keep, and is in season. If there's doubt, get the fish in as soon as you can so as to tire it the least. If you mistake a large enough fish for one that's too small, you can always decide to keep it. But if you exhaust a fish and then realize it's too small to keep, it's too late.

If you're using light or ultra-light tackle, be it conventional, spin or fly, with the full intention of releasing whatever you catch, understand there will be times you'll catch a fish larger than expected and will have to break the fish off. Better to let the fish worry about getting rid of the hook than to tire it beyond recovery. To break off a fish, simply take a turn or two of line around the handle of your reel, point the rod directly at the fish and let the fish do the rest. With no drag or rod bend to absorb shock, the line will break, usually at the leader knot.

Finally, avoid multiple hooks when using bait, and never use bait for catch-and-release fishing. For some species, use of multiple (e.g., treble) hooks with bait is illegal. For any species you're going to release, it's unwise. It isn't really necessary anyway, so why risk injuring the fish?

Catch-and-release fishing can be a great deal of fun. There's no worry about bag limits or closed seasons, and if done properly, no concern for size. If you get into a school of undersized fish, use of light tackle can turn a so-so day into a memorable one. Just apply some common sense and consideration for your quarry and have a ball.

One If By Net, Two If By Hand

There are many ways to take advantage of Florida's abundant marine life without a rod and reel. In season, lobsters, oysters, and scallops can be harvested by simply picking them up. All year long there are blue claw crabs, and during the summer months shrimp are easily netted from bridges, piers, and boats.

Bay Scallops

From April 1 through June 30, you can take up to five gallons of whole scallops, or one-half gallon of whole meat, which is a mess of scallops. There are special regulations in effect for St. Joe Bay in the Panhandle, and some gear restrictions apply. Check with local officials before you go after these tasty treats.

Scallops are generally harvested in shallow water, and the only gear needed is a diving flag, a face mask, and a mesh bag to hold your harvest.

All you need to do is stick your head in the water and look on the bottom. The addition of a snorkel will of course add to the time you can search, but it isn't really needed. One thing often overlooked is the dive flag. Although you are merely wading, because of the need to submerge to pick up scallops, you must have a "diver down" flag displayed to alert boaters.

Crabs

There are several ways to collect blue claw crabs. First, there is the traditional collapsible crab trap, which can be used effectively from a bridge, dock, or fishing pier. You cannot use more than five traps without a permit from the Department of Environmental Protection (DEP). Crabs are abundant in most of the canals along both coasts, and can frequently be captured with a dip net. In some places they are so numerous you can simply walk along the bank of a canal and scoop them up as you see them.

But they aren't that numerous everywhere in the state, and in most places a bit more preparation is called for. For most crabbing, some kind of bait is needed. One good method is to make a ring of a piece of metal—a coat hanger will do, but a piece of light aluminum stock will last longer—and thread small fish or pieces of meat onto it. Tie a line to the ring, immerse it in the water until you feel a crab playing with the bait, then slowly raise it until you can see the crab and slip a net under it.

Various methods are employed in placing small baitfish on the hook. Some go through the tail, some through both lips, and others through the back, just below the dorsal fin. All will work. Instead of fish, you can also use various meats such as chicken parts. What's left over after you clean fish also makes excellent crab bait.

Stone crabs are harvested in an entirely different matter. Only the claws are taken, and the live crab must then be returned to the water. (They will regenerate the claw.) Claws cannot be removed from egg-bearing females. The same gear restrictions apply as for crawfish. The claw must measure 2¾ inches in length, and the season is closed from May 15 and October 15.

Crawfish

Often called Florida lobsters, the spiny lobster is a delicious, if smaller, version of the lobsters found in northern waters. The carapace must measure at least 3 inches, and if you don't know how to measure that, you need to do some research before you go after what Floridians affectionately refer to as "bugs." It would be a simple matter for me to explain how to measure a crawfish, but my point is if you are that inexperienced, you need to talk with other divers in your particular area, as lobster regulations are quite complex and strictly enforced. You must have a carapace measuring device in your possession while hunting lobsters.

Crawfish must remain in whole condition until landed. Crawfish season is closed from April 1 through August 5 and there is a limit of 24 per boat or 6 per person, whichever is greater. A crawfish stamp is required, and you cannot trap them. Crawfish can be harvested only by hand or with a bully net. The use of grains, spears, hooks, or similar devices is prohibited.

The last consecutive Wednesday and Thursday of July is set aside as a sport fisherman's day, and commercial harvest is not allowed on those days. Harvest methods are limited and bag limits vary by day and area within the state. Check with the Marine Patrol or an experienced diver for the regulations in your area.

Oysters

Many oyster bars are completely exposed part of the time, so oysters tightly shut their shells to exclude heat and air, and to retain moisture. As the tide floods the bars, the oysters open and resume feeding, filtering organisms from the water. (It's interesting to note that oysters transported 1,000 miles inland continued to open and close according to the tidal schedule at their place of origin for several weeks, gradually adapting to open at the time of high tide at their new location.)

Because of this filtering activity, oysters do much to keep the water clean and clear. However, you should keep in mind many organisms filtered out of the water by oysters are poisonous to humans, especially if the oysters are consumed raw. Consequently, there are many sections of the state in which harvest of oysters is prohibited at any time. Because they are unable to move about, oysters, clams, most mussels, and some scallops are among the first animals to be affected by pollution. Eating contaminated oysters, especially raw, can be fatal. Take no chances. If you plan to harvest shellfish, check not only that you're in the proper season, but also that you aren't in one of the restricted areas.

Even in areas where oyster harvest is normally permitted, heavy rains can cause temporary shutdowns. When tropical storm Alberto dumped its enormous load of rain on the southwestern part of Georgia in 1994, the resulting river floods caused a complete shutdown of oyster harvesting in Florida's Apalachicola Bay, into which those rivers flow. Don't go strictly by published maps showing where harvest is permitted; it's important to have up-to-date information.

Marine Patrol officers and local bait and tackle shops are excellent sources for this information. You could also telephone the outdoor editor of a local newspaper, but it probably wouldn't help, as he'd be out fishing. Letters, however, usually will bring a response.

Oysters must measure 3 inches across, but that's the end of the simple rules for oyster harvesting. Beyond that, the times and areas when harvesting is permitted are so complex the only recourse you have is to check with the Marine Patrol with specific information on where and when you want to take oysters to determine whether or not it will be permitted. Basically, at this writing, oyster season is closed during June, July, and August in Dixie and Levy Counties (on the Gulf Coast just south of the Big Bend area) and during July, August, and September in the rest of the state.

Shrimp

During the summer months large numbers of shrimp migrate from the grass flats out to the ocean and Gulf of Mexico, on the outgoing tide. Shrimpers hang lights such as Coleman lanterns from bridges and use long-handled dip nets to scoop them up as they are swept beneath the bridge. Nights near the full moon are best, as the tide runs more swiftly. Boaters also use lights and a shorter net to gather the shrimp.

The limit is five gallons of whole shrimp per day per person *or vessel.*

Shrimp, especially small ones, can also be seined by pushing a small-mesh net through grass beds, but this method is not at all efficient if you're after large, eating-sizes shrimp.

Summary

Be sure you know the regulations, and follow them. It will save you the heartache of learning belatedly that you have violated the law, and perhaps a hefty fine as well. One thing about information on fishing regulations is that it's easy to come by, and free. Take a few minutes to become familiar with applicable laws and regulations, and carry measuring devices and, if necessary, fish identification guides with you at all times.

Above all, have fun.

Good Fighting
or Good
Table Fare?

Fishing for Fight and Food

There are many fish in the inshore waters of Florida that are great fighters. There are also many that are delicious. Several species are both. The emphasis here is on those that are not all that satisfying as a meal, to save you from being disappointed and having to take your spouse on an unplanned dinner date. But we'll get to the good guys, too. (Many Florida restaurants will cook your catch for you, especially if the restaurant is associated with the motel or hotel at which you're staying; they're used to being asked, so don't be shy.)

The list won't be all-inclusive. No attempt will be made to name every fish that can't or shouldn't be eaten, or that can and should be. What the list will include are just those that are not only numerous, but also enjoy a wide range, being found through-out most or all of the state.

I'll preface this discourse with a disclaimer. Many fish, while quite edible, require special or tedious preparation before cooking. Ladyfish, tarpon, and bonefish are examples. Others can be poisonous, such as barracuda. I'll explain in a minute. Strictly speaking, most fish are edible. For our purposes, however, read "edible" as "worth the trouble to prepare, and tasty." Anything else will be considered inedible.

Notable among inedible scrappers are barracuda, bonefish, jack crevalle (properly "crevalle jack"), ladyfish, and tarpon. It's interesting to note that for the first few hundred years of Florida's settlement by clever and civilized folks, snook would have been included in that list, being considered fare for only the lowly poor who couldn't get "good" fish. They were, in fact, known for some time as "soapfish" for the strong oily flavor of their flesh and the fact that pounding the skin while it's wet produces a soapy foam. Then the poor folks took pity and explained that snook *must* be

Figure 11-1. Phil Saul and Capt. Greenan with a nice snook that hit a topwater plug in Bull Bay, on the southwest Gulf Coast. Note the relative size of head and mouth to the body.

skinned before cooking. The difference is nothing short of amazing. Skinned, snook are among the tastiest of all fish.

The simplest way to skin snook is to use two knives, one sharp, one not. Use the sharp knife to cut filets. Turn the filet over so the skin side is down. Make a small incision to but not through the skin, at the tail end. Place the dull knife in this incision, angled slightly up from horizontal. Grasp the base of the filet with the empty hand and pull back while pushing forward with the knife hand. You may find it helpful to wiggle the skin as you pull. With a little practice, you'll soon have completely skin-free filets every time. While this will also work with other species, the thick skins of redfish and snook make it particularly effective. It's much more difficult with species such as spotted seatrout, which have thin, easily-cut skin.

The species previously named as inedible (all can be eaten, but special knowledge and care are needed to make them palatable) are all terrific fighters. Barracuda are not strictly inedible. Properly prepared, in fact, they are quite good. However, when feeding on certain species of fish, they can be poisonous (the disease, which is called "ciguatera", can be fatal); so it's best you return them to the water until you have enough experience to know when and in which sections of the state they're safe to eat.

Bonefish and tarpon, of course, have been written about so often there's no need to go into their fighting ability here. Suffice it to say they will give you your money's worth. Ladyfish are related to tarpon and the fact is they apparently think they *are* tarpon. Their method of losing you is the same; take to the air. As they are much smaller, they lack the stamina of tarpon, but the fight, while comparatively short-lived, will be spectacular nevertheless.

Yes, there are several species of shark that can be and are caught close to shore. Examples are bonnethead, bull, nurse, and sharpnose. All are generally taken on bait, often while fishing for something else. Most are small for sharks, but all are powerful fighters, and care should be taken when releasing them, as with all sharks.

Jack crevalle employ a different strategy, and it's important to understand this. Jacks depend on brute strength and incredible stamina. They hit hard and immediately head somewhere else,

Figure 11-2. Even small jack crevalle will give a good account of themselves on light tackle. This one hit a Baby Zara Spook on a noodle rod and 4-lb-test line.

and unlike some of the glamor species, it isn't a case of one good run. They run, you work them back to you, they say "No, I don't wanna do that," and take off again. It's not uncommon to get a half-dozen long runs from a jack crevalle.

It's important to know this, because you can and will kill jacks unnecessarily if you fish for them with tackle that's too light. At some point, when the fish is obviously beginning to falter, you must quit the fight and bring them in so they can be released before they get exhausted beyond recovery.

Studies, notably by the Sea Grant Foundation at Cornell University, have determined that during a battle, lactic acid builds up in the tissues of a fish. That acid must be dissipated relatively quickly if full recovery is to take place, and the longer the fight and the buildup continue, the less likely such recovery is. When deliberately fishing for jack crevalle or for edible species you intend to release—redfish and snook out of season, for example—keep in mind that at some point you may have to stop letting the fish run and haul it in, and be sure your tackle is capable of doing it.

Of course, we can't always anticipate what will hit, and I've often found myself with a fish—usually a jack—that I wanted to horse in and couldn't, most often while using 2- or 4-lb-test line. In such a case, there's only one good option; break off the fish. Better to lose a hook or a lure than to kill a fish needlessly. Taking it home to bury it under the roses may be better than simply tossing a dead fish back, but it's so much a better choice to not kill it in the first place.

The only good reason to kill a fish today is because you're going to eat it. It isn't even necessary, with today's procedures, to kill a fish for a mount. Most good taxidermists can and regularly do make quite believable "mounts" from nothing more than a photograph and the pertinent measurements, and they last longer than traditional fish skin mounts.

Fish are usually considered inedible because of a preponderance of bones. This is the case with ladyfish, bonefish, and tarpon. In others, such as jack crevalle, the flesh is just too oily and strong to be good table fare. There are those who do eat jacks, however, usually simmering them in a small amount of water, discarding the water and replacing it with fresh water two or even three times. Generally, the flesh is then used for a fish chowder or stew. If you prefer a pronounced fishy taste over milder flavor, you might want to give jack chowder a try.

Many edible species are not unique to Florida. If you live on any of the nation's coasts, you're probably familiar with flounder (there are three types in Florida—summer, Gulf, and Atlantic—all roughly the size of the common winter flounder found in the northeastern U.S.), drum (both black drum and red drum, the latter also known as channel bass or redfish), whiting (known in the northeast as kingfish); croakers; and the various weakfish and seatrouts.

In the winter, Floridians enjoy the same bluefish that cruise most of the east U.S. coast during summer months, and mackerel are found on both Florida coasts at various times. During the warmer months, cobia will prowl the flats looking for a meal, and, in the Panhandle area, even small bonito can be found inshore when the water warms. At the longest pier in the state (some claim it's the longest on the entire Gulf coast), located in Panama City Beach, bonito, cobia, and king mackerel are regularly taken during warmer months.

Identification of the various species is not generally difficult. However, three easily and frequently confused fish are jack crevalle, permit, and pompano. All are members of the broad *Carangidae* (jacks and pompanos) family. Of the three, the jack crevalle is the easiest to identify. Near the tail, along the side of the fish, are small bony projections called "scutes." Neither permit, nor pompano have scutes, so their presence is an immediate and simple identification for the jack.

Distinguishing between permit and pompano, especially in the smaller sizes, can be tricky, but there are several clues for which you can look. Pompano rarely exceed 6 pounds, while permit grow much larger, with 40-lb fish not uncommon. Small permit can resemble pompano quite closely, but there are two major tip-offs. First, the permit's back slants sharply downward at the second dorsal fin, and the fish is much deeper in body shape. Second, the pompano has a much larger area of yellow shading its body near the throat and the anal and pelvic fins. If you have the time and want to get into it, the permit has 17 to 21 soft dorsal rays, while the pompano has from 20 to 23, and the soft anal rays number 16 to 19 and 20 to 23, respectively.

While there are great scrappers not mentioned here, those that are mentioned are found throughout the state, although not, perhaps, year-round. Tarpon can be found anywhere in the state during the summer months, but only in the southern half for much of the year. Jacks, while more numerous at some times than at others, are everywhere all the time. Ladyfish can likewise generally be found just about anywhere, especially during the warmer months. While occasionally caught as far north as Fort Pierce, bonefish are generally restricted to the southern parts of the state.

All will take artificials, as well as shrimp. Tarpon will readily take crabs, and this is the preferred method for those schools traveling along the beaches, especially on the west coast. Hook the crab through one of the side points, as shown in Chapter 2. A common way to take these fish is to sight them as they move par-

Figure 11-3. Moments before, this member of the "Manasota Mob" had been in a daisy chain with other gang members, but luckily for me it took time out to snack on a live crab cast to the edge of the school.

allel to the beach, wait until they pause and form a moving circle (this is called a "daisy chain," for the manner in which the fish follow each other nose to tail), and put the crab where it can be seen. (See Chapter 8.)

A Few Ways to Enjoy Your Catch

All in all, Florida's inshore waters offer a plethora of hard-fighting fish that can be taken on a variety of artificial and natural baits. That some of them also provide an excellent meal is a bonus for which those of us who fish the skinny water are ever grateful. To help along those lines, here are a few recipes from Mark Weintz, who not only knows how to catch them, but what to do with them when he gets them home. Mark writes the "Sportsman's Kitchen" column monthly for *Florida Sportsman* magazine.

For a mess of whiting on a grill. (Many Florida shore side parks have grills.)

6 or 8 scaled, gutted and headed whiting
1 stick of butter, melted
1-3 cloves of garlic, minced
2 tbsp onion, finely chopped
1 lemon cut in wedges
2 stalks of celery with leaves
4 oz block Parmesan cheese, grated
Dash of black pepper

Combine butter, garlic, and onion. Squeeze one lemon wedge into mixture. Use celery leaves as a basting brush for the butter. Also brush grill just before putting on the fish. A wire fish basket helps prevent sticking and makes it easy to turn all the fish at one time.

Grill fish over high heat, uncovered. Turn fish after six minutes, basting before and after turning. Fish should be done in about 10 to 15 minutes, depending on the grill and the size of the catch. When done, fish will be opaque, juicy, and will flake easily at the thickest point. But the best way to tell when fish is done is to pull gently on a dorsal fin. When the fin pulls out easily, you're ready to dig in.

During the last minute of grilling, cover the top of the fish with the grated cheese. Serve with remaining butter sauce and cheese.

Here's a good one for spotted seatrout called "Nutty Trout Gone Bananas":

3 lbs seatrout fillets
4 tbsp melted butter (the real stuff)
3 tbsp Amaretto
1 green banana
1 yellow banana
Salt & pepper to taste
Flour for dredging fillets
Slivered almonds

Preheat oven to 450°F. Dredge fillets and season with salt and pepper. Pour half the butter in the baking dish and grate 3 tbsp. of green banana into the dish. Add the fish. Put three more tbsp. grated green banana on top of the fish. Slice ripe banana lengthwise and put one half on each filet. Sprinkle fish with slivered almonds. Drizzle Amaretto and remaining butter over the fish. Bake for 10 or 15 minutes, basting a couple of times with juice. Fish is done when it is opaque and flakes easily. Serve with rice, potatoes or nothing at all.

Here are two that will work with most any kind of fillets:

"Double Dressing Fish"
Fish fillets
Blue cheese dressing
Mayonnaise

Mix equal amounts of blue cheese dressing and mayonnaise-enough to smother the fillets. Spoon half the dressing mix into a baking pan. Put fillets in pan and cover with remaining dressing. Bake at 400°F for 10 minutes for each half-inch thickness of the fillets. To reduce the calories and fat you can use low-fat mayonnaise and blue cheese dressing.

"Peppered Fillets"
1 lb fillets
1 tbsp butter, melted
3 cloves garlic, minced
1 onion, chopped
Black peppercorns
Pepper mill

Lightly oil a baking pan and place the fillets into it. Pour butter over fish and add garlic and onions. Grind pepper over the entire dish, making a one-eighth inch thick coating. Bake at 400°F for 10 minutes for each 1-inch thickness of fish. This recipe cooks more quickly than the one above due to the lack of dressing.
Enjoy.

Guides and Facilities

Any article, book, or treatise on professional fishing guides and marinas must by its very nature be unfair to someone. Especially in such a fishing- and boating-oriented state as Florida, it would be impossible to include all the good ones. Consequently, I must emphasize that not being included in my list in no way implies a person or facility is second-rate. But I have not gone by word-of-mouth. Instead, I have listed here guides with whom I have personal experience, and marinas I've used. I've tried to include additional information where it was pertinent.

You can also contact Ralph Delligatti, Florida Guides Association, 6023 26th Street W., Suite 101, Bradenton, FL 34207, (telephone 813-756-4304) for the name of a guide in any particular area. Two other sources are: Florida Inshore Sportfishing Association, Inc., P.O. Box 1536, New Smyrna Beach, FL 32170-1536 (President Stanley Clavet, 904-428-8208, Vice President Leo Hiles, 904-345-2213) and Saltwater Flats & Fly Fishing Association, 415 24th Street North, St. Petersburg, FL 33713.

The guides are listed alphabetically.

Captain Phil Chapman
6882 Hayter Drive
Lakeland, FL 33813
813-646-9445

(Chapman is not only an excellent fly fisherman, but is also a fisheries biologist. Fishes primarily the Gulf Coast from Homosassa north. Tarpon a specialty.)

Captain James Davenport
Cedar Key
904-543-9323
(Also marine service & repairs.)

Captain Gregg Gentile
Martin and St. Lucie County areas (east coast)
407-878-0475
(Light tackle specialist, especially the Loxahatchee River, St. Lucie River, and Indian River Lagoon.)

Captain Steve Graf
Steinhatchee, FL 32359
904-776-1041
(Light tackle specialist, including fly tackle.)

Captain Peter Greenan
2416 Parsons Lane
Sarasota, FL 34239
813-925-9483 or 813-923-6095
(Fishes Charlotte Harbor and Boca Grande areas mostly, but also Everglades and Ten Thousand Islands. Light tackle specialist, including fly tackle. Also gives fly tying and fly casting clinics.)

Captain Paul Hawkins
P.O. Box 7005
St. Petersburg, FL 33734
813-825-2882
(Fly fishing specialist.)

Captain Van Hubbard
P.O. Box 821
Boca Grande, FL 33921
813-697-6944
(Also an outdoor writer and TV show host.)

Captain Roger Johnson
900 S. Rooks Avenue
Inverness, FL 32650
904-344-5765
(Also guides in fresh water.)

Captain Greg Koon
P.O. Box 8023
Port St. Lucie, FL 34985
407-879-9751

Captain Mike Locklear
P.O. Box 900
Homosassa, FL 32687
904-628-4207
(Light tackle and fly tackle specialist. Also gives seminars and instruction. Fishes Homosassa flats.)

Captain Larry Mendez
3601 S. Westshore Blvd.
Tampa, FL 33629
813-837-9573
(Despite the Tampa address, Mendez also fishes extensively in the Charlotte Harbor area.)

Captain Chris Mitchell
P.O. Box 1046
Tarpon Street
Boca Grande, FL 33921
813-964-2887

Captain Terry Moore
P.O. Box 24
Steinhatchee, FL 32359
904-498-3877

Captain Abbie Napier
No. 7 First Street
Cedar Key, FL 904-543-5511
(Specializing in spotted seatrout and offshore fishing.)

Captain Alec Williams
P.O. Box 215
Homosassa, FL 32646
904-628-3024 or 904-498-3944
(Also provides cooked shore lunches.)

Captain James Wood, Sr.
P.O. Box 224
Terra Ceia, FL 34250
813-722-5746
(Terra Ceia is on the Gulf Coast, near the St. Petersburg/Tampa area.)

Facilities and Marinas

In major metropolitan areas, marinas abound, and to try to list them would be counterproductive. Instead, here are a few that provide multiple services, and with which I have personal experience.

Angler's Resort
P.O. Box 77
Suwannee, FL 32692
904-542-7077
Rooms, restaurants, guides etc. all available in one spot where the Suwannee empties into the Gulf of Mexico. Excellent fishing for redfish, seatrout and, in season, cobia. Also a great place for scallops in season.

Boca Grande North
P.O. Box 1043
Boca Grande, FL 33921
800-962-3314
While not a fishing facility, Boca Grande North is located in a great area and there are guides nearby. Efficiency apartments are for rent, and there is a permanent dock where your guide can pick you up. If you trail your own boat, you can tie up at the dock. There are the usual amenities for non-anglers such as a swimming pool. This is an excellent place to stay.

Ideal Fish Camp
P.O. Box 24
Steinhatchee, FL 32359
904-498-3877
Boats, motors, bait, guides, and so on. Also has a dock with a boat lift for in-and-out service.

Macrae's Bait House
P.O. Box 318
Homosassa, FL 34487
904-628-2602
Macrae's has efficiency cabins for rent, bait, guides, etc. The owners donated their launching ramp to the county, so there is no fee to use it. There are also johnboats and pontoon boats for rent. Macrae's is right on a river, with quick access to the Gulf.

Miller's Marina
P.O. Box 715
Boca Grande, FL 33921
813-964-2232

Rosemeyer's Boat Rental
3281 NE Indian River Drive
Jensen Beach, FL 34957
407-334-1000
Boat and tackle rental in the midst of great redfish, snook, and trout country. All boats equipped with VHF radios.

Uncle Henry's Marina
P.O. Box 294
Boca Grande, FL 33921
813-964-2300
This is an excellent facility, offering rooms, restaurants, a lounge, and slips for large and small boats. Dockmaster monitors VHF Channel 16. Uncle Henry's can also arrange for guides, both inshore and offshore, and some of the best guides in the area work out of this marina.

The Lee County Visitor and Convention Bureau compiled an extensive list of facilities that offer boat and tackle rental, guide services, etc. The list includes Captiva and Sanibel Isalnds, Fort Myers Beach, Fort Myers, Cape Coral, Bonita Springs, North Fort Myers, Pine Island and Boca Grande. Write or call for a copy of the list.

Lee County Visitor and Convention Bureau
P.O. Box 2445
Fort Myers, FL 33902-2445
800-533-4753

Get yourself a guide, get out there and enjoy the finest skinny water fishing there is, along the inshore waters of Florida. It's an experience you won't forget.

Warning: It's addictive.

Information Sources

Regulatory Agencies

Florida Marine Patrol
Marjory Stoneman Douglas Building
3900 Commonwealth Boulevard
Tallahassee, FL 32399-3000
Voice: 904-488-5757
FAX: 907-487-4590
To report fishing violations or suspicious activity, you can call toll-free to 800-342-5367 (800-DIALFMP).
When writing the Marine Patrol, allow plenty of time. (As an example, at this writing I'm still awaiting a reply to a question about which I've written twice in three months.)

Florida Department of Environmental Protection (DER)
3900 Commonwealth Boulevard
Tallahassee, FL 32399-3000
904-488-7326
This department is responsible for enforcing fishing regulations through the Florida Marine Patrol, as well as conducting marine research and improving fisheries habitat.

Local Agencies

Many areas of Florida have agencies responsible for providing information to tourists and new or potential residents. Some are listed here, starting in the northeast section and working around the Keys and back up the Gulf side to the Panhandle. County names and titles such as "The Nature Coast" may have little meaning for those not familiar with Florida geography, so where it would be helpful I have added the name of a major city, a well known fishing town or the general geographic area covered. Don't use anything in italics as part of the address.

If you'd like information about an area not covered, contact the Florida Department of Tourism in Tallahassee, at 904-488-8230.

Northeast coast above St. Augustine
Clay County Tourist Development Council
477 Houston Street
Post Office Box 1366
Green Cove Springs, FL 32043
Voice: 904-284-6300
FAX: 904-278-4731

St. Augustine/St. Johns County Tourist Dev. Council
One Riberia Street
St. Augustine, FL 32084
Voice: 904-829-5681
FAX: 904-829-6477

Ponte Vedra Beach south to Matanzas Inlet
St. Johns County Tourist Development Council
10 Castillo Drive
St. Augustine, FL 32084
or
Post Office Box 349
St. Augustine, FL 32085
Voice: 904-823-2419

Titusville, Cocoa, Melbourne area, including the Merritt Island National Wildlife Refuge
Space Coast Office of Tourism

and
Brevard County Tourist Development Council
2725 St. Johns Street, Building C
Melbourne, FL 32940
Voice: 407-633-2110
FAX: 407-633-2112

Sebastian Inlet to just south of Vero Beach
The Tourism Council, Chamber of Commerce
1216 21st Street
Vero Beach, FL 32960
Voice: 407-567-3491
FAX: 407-778-3181

From north of Fort Pierce Inlet to just north of Jensen Beach, and the heart of the Indian River Lagoon.
St. Lucie County Tourist Development Council
2300 Virginia Avenue
Fort Pierce, FL 34982
Voice: 407-462-1529
or 800-344-TGIF
FAX: 407-462-2132

Greater Fort Lauderdale Convention & Visitors Bureau
200 East Las Olas Boulevard, Suite 1500
Fort Lauderdale, FL 33301
Voice: 305-765-4466
FAX: 305-765-4467

Greater Miami Convention & Visitors Bureau
701 Brickell Avenue, Suite 2700
Miami, FL 33131
Voice: 305-539-3084
FAX: 305-539-3113

The Florida Keys
Monroe County Tourist Development Council
3406 North Roosevelt Boulevard, Suite 201
Key West, FL 33040
Voice: 305-296-1552 or

800-648-5510 (from Florida or 202 area code only)
FAX: 305-296-0788

Another source of information for the Keys is:
Stuart Newman Associates
3191 Coral Way
Miami, FL 33145
Voice: 305-461-3300 or
800-ASK-KEYS
FAX: 305-461-3311
Compuserve: 71055,1357

Charlotte Harbor, including Boca Grande
Lee County Visitor & Convention Bureau
2180 West First Street, Suite 100
Fort Myers, FL 33901
Voice: 941-338-3500 or
800-237-6444
FAX: 941-334-1106

Sarasota Convention & Visitors Bureau
655 North Tamiami Trail
Sarasota, FL 34236
Voice: 941-957-1877
FAX: 941-951-2956

Bradenton Area Convention & Visitors Bureau
Post Office Box 1000
Bradenton, FL 34206
Voice: 941-729-9177 or 800-822-2017
FAX: 941-729-1820

St. Petersburg/Clearwater Convention and Visitors Bureau
Thunder Dome
One Stadium Drive, Suite A
St. Petersburg, FL 33705
Voice: 813-892-7892
FAX: 813-582-7949

Tampa/Hillsborough Convention & Visitor Association
111 Madison Street, Suite 1010

Tampa, FL 33602
Voice: 813-223-1111, extension 52
FAX: 813-229-6616

Port Richey
Pasco County Tourist Development Council
7530 Little Road
New Port Richey, FL 34654
Voice: 813-847-8990 or 800-842-1873
FAX: 813-847-8969

Hernando County Tourism Development Council
16110 Aviation Loop Drive
Brooksville, FL 34609
Voice: 904-799-7275
FAX: 904-799-1711

Crystal River, Homosassa Springs
Citrus County Tourist Development Council
1300 South Lecanto Highway
Lecanto, FL 34461
Voice: 904-746-4223
FAX: 904-746-5869

Cedar Key
Levy County Tourist Development Council
612 East Hathaway Avenue
Bronson, FL 32621
Voice: 904-486-3006
FAX: 904-486-6262

The Big Bend area, the start of Florida's Panhandle.
Taylor County Coastal Association
Route 2, Box 130
Keaton Beach, FL 32347
Voice: 904-578-2637

Tallahassee Area Visitors Information Center
200 West College Avenue, Suite 302
Tallahassee, FL 32302
Voice: 904-488-3990 or 800-628-2866
FAX: 904-487-4621

Panama City area, including St. Andrews State Park
Bay County Convention & Visitors Bureau
12015 Front Beach Road
Panama City Beach, FL 32407 or Post Office Box 9473
Panama City Beach, FL 32417
Voice: 904-233-5070 or 800-PCBEACH
FAX: 904-233-5072

Destin, Santa Rosa area; western Florida Panhandle
South Walton Tourist Development Council
Highway 98, Emerald Coast Plaza, Unit 37
Post Office Box 1248
Santa Rosa Beach, FL 32459
Voice: 904-267-1216
FAX: 904-267-3943

Choctawhatchee Bay, Fort Walton Beach
Emerald Coast Convention & Visitors Bureau
Post Office Box 609
Fort Walton Beach, FL 32549-0609
Voice: 904-651-7131 or 800-322-3319
FAX: 904-651-7149

Almost Alabama
Pensacola Convention & Visitors Information Center
1401 East Gregory Street
Pensacola, FL 32501
Voice: 904-434-1234 or 800-874-1234 (US)
800-343-4321 (FL)
FAX: 904-432-8211

Manufacturers

Here are addresses and telephone numbers for many of the manufacturers of the lines, lures, and other products mentioned in this book. Contact them for any additional information. Some are now on CompuServe Information Service (CIS), and where applicable, I have included their User ID (CompuServe address).

If your tackle shop doesn't carry the barbless hooks from O. Mustad & Son, they can be ordered. You want model #35524N. If you aren't sure what size the hooks you're replacing are, be sure to take one with you as a sample. If you have no way to get them locally, you can order them through the following:

Merrick Tackle Center, Inc.   Tim's Tackle Box
Attention Scott Greenberg   1505 East Michigan Street
7349 Route 28, HC 2   Orlando, FL 32806
Shandaken, NY 12480   407-894-5404
800-628-8904

Bluewater Tackle   Captain Harry's Fishing Supply
100460 Overseas Highway   100 N.E. 11th Street
Key Largo, FL 33037   Miami, FL 33132
305-451-5875   305-374-4661

Abu-Garcia, makers of Pro Max, Black Max and Cardinal Spinning reels, Ambassadeur baitcasting reels and an extensive line of graphite rods:

Abu-Garcia   The Walker Agency
21 Law Drive   15855 N. Greenway-Hayden Loop
Fairfield, NJ   or   Suite 160
07004-3296   Scottsdale, AZ 85260
201-227-7666   602-483-0185
    CompuServe: 76167,301

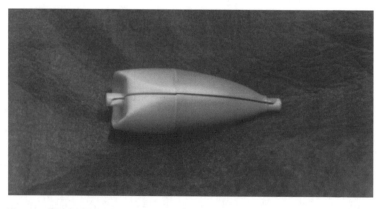

Figure A2-1. The red and green Alameda Popping Float snaps on and off the line easily and comes in 5 sizes, with and without a rattle.

Alameda Fishing Tackle Co. makes a unique plastic popping
"cork" in several sizes with and without a rattle.
Alameda Fishing Tackle Co.
P.O. Box 7071
Corpus Christi, TX 78415
512-855-7437

Berkley, makers of a wide variety of fishing lines, including
Gorilla braided line, Trilene, Big Game and other monofila-
ment lines, fly lines, fly reels, all types of rods, a line of lures
and accessories for anglers:
Berkley Consumer Services
One Berkley Drive
Spirit Lake, IA 51360
712-336-1520

Bill Lewis Lures, makers of both floating and sinking Rat-L-Trap,
the Spitfire topwater bait and other lures effective in Florida,
many in saltwater versions:
Bill Lewis Lures
P.O. Box 7959
Alexandria, LA 71306-0959
318-487-0352

Cotee Bait Company makes the Liv'Eye Action Jig and the Rattlin' Liv'Eye Jigs, a spoon, a soft topwater bait and some very
effective enhancers to encourage hits. The enhancers include
ProBait Tip-it and ProBait Chunk-it, the difference being size.
Cotee also makes Bait Shapes, a natural product that can be
used alone or added to a jig or other lure:
Cotee Bait Company, Inc.
6045 Sherwin Drive
Port Richey, FL 34668
813-845-3737 or 800-776-2248

DEHOOKER makes a device in two designs (one for mouth-
hooked fish and one for fish hooked deeper), which makes
releasing fish not only simpler but less likely to cause harm to
the fish, often without removing it from the water:

Dehooker, Inc.
5928 N. Oceanshore Blvd.
Palm Coast, FL 32137
800-772-5804

Daiwa manufactures a line of rods and reels much in use in saltwater and fresh:
Daiwa Corporation
7421 Chapman Avenue
Garden Grove, CA 92641
Voice: 714-895-6645

D.O.A. makes a line of quite lifelike soft plastic imitations of baitfish, crabs and shrimp effective on most Florida species that will take artificial baits:
D.O.A. Fishing Lures
3461-B Palm City School Ave.
Palm City, FL 34990
407-287-5001

Dana Griffin offers a line of saltwater flies tied specifically for inshore Florida species as well as "traditional" flies. For a catalog, write:
Florida Fly Tyer
3859 NW 32 Place
Gainesville, FL 32606

Doelcher introduced the first, and what many say is the best, hydrofoil addition for outboard motors as an aid in getting up on plane more quickly and to prevent porpoising; it's called the Doel Fin Hydrofoil.
Doelcher Products
2970 Bay Vista Court
Unit A
Benicia, CA 94510
707-745-3488 or 800-422-2205

Kodiak Scent Company has a line of attractants in various oils, pastes, soaks and powders, some of which target saltwater species with anchovy, ballyhoo (balao), herring, mullet, shrimp, and squid scents:

Kodiak Scent Company
725 Broadway Avenue
Bedford, OH 44146
216-232-8352

Love's Lures offers tandem jig rigs in a wide selection of size and color:
Love's Lures
6855 George M. Lynch Drive N.
St. Petersburg, FL 33702
800-866-5447

Mann's Bait Company manufactures many fine lures and accessories which work well in Florida, including the Loudmouth series of jerkbait.
Mann's Bait Company
604 State Docks Road
Eufaula, AL 36027

Mann's Spare Hand

Figure A2-2. The Spare Hand belt-mounted rod holder from Mann's Bait Company frees your hands for changing baits, releasing fish, or tying knots while wading.

205-687-5716

FAX: 205-687-4352

MirrOlures have been catching fish in inshore Florida waters for more than forty years, and are favorites for several species, holding records for trout in a number of line classes, including nearly a dozen fish exceeding 12 pounds, all but 3 of which were caught in Florida:

L&S Bait Company, Inc.

1415 East Bay Drive

Largo, FL 34641

813-584-7691

FAX: 813-587-0784

Penn Fishing Tackle, long-time maker of excellent reels, most of which are suitable for saltwater.

Penn Fishing Tackle Mfg. Co.

3028 W. Hunting Park Avenue

Philadelphia, PA 19132

215-229-9415

Plano Molding Company makes tackle boxes, including the Tackle Racker mentioned in Chapter Eight:

Plano Molding Company

431 E. South Street

Plano, IL 60545-1601

708-552-3111

FAX: 708-552-9737

PRADCO: See end of manufacturers listing.

Rugged Gear manufactures sturdy gun and rod holders which are corrosionproof. They can be mounted by strong suction cups, an adhesive strip or screws.

Rugged Gear

200 Eagle Lane

RR 1, Box 2B

Elk Point, SD 57025

800-784-4331

FAX: 605-356-2330

Sawyer Products manufactures various insect repellents and treatments for insect bites and toxic plant contact as well as sun block and burn treatments:
Sawyer Products
P.O. Box 188
Safety Harbor, FL 34695
800-356-7811

Scientific Anglers has many fly lines suitable for use in inshore Florida, and its Mastery Series includes floating and sinking fly lines in Bonefish, Saltwater and Tarpon tapers, simplifying line selection:
Scientific Anglers
3M Center, Building 223-4NE-05
St. Paul, MN 55144-1000
800-525-6290

Shakespeare, manufacturers of rods, reels and accessories.
Shakespeare Fishing Tackle
3801 Westmore Drive
Columbia, SC 29223
803-754-7000 or 800-334-9105

Shimano rods & reels:
P.O. Box 19615
One Shimano Drive
Irvine, CA 92713-9615
800-833-5540

Solo Systems offers a unique weedless lure that can be walked over oysters or cast with near impunity into tangled mangrove roots.
Solo Systems, Inc.
6235 (Box C) 118th Avenue N.
Largo, FL 34643
800-226-4055

Storm Lures, in addition to a line of good plugs, offers the SuspenDot system, whereby adhesive-backed, weighted decals allow you to alter the buoyancy of lures to change the level at which they will suspend in the water:

Storm Lures
P.O. Box 720265
Norman, OK 73070-4199
405-329-5894

Stren lines, long a favorite of anglers, now includes a braided line in a low-visibility green:
Stren Fishing Lines
Delle Conne Corporate Center
1011 Centre Road
Wilmington, DE 19805
800-243-9700

Tender Corporation manufactures a complete line of outdoor protection and relief products.
Tender Corporation
P.O. Box 290
Littleton Industrial Park
Littleton, NH 03561
603-444-5464 or 800-258-4696

For information on Bomber, Cordell (Pencil Popper), Creek Chub, Heddon (Zara Spook, Dying Flutter), Rebel (Pop-R, Jumpin' Minnow), and Riverside (Real Baitfish), contact *Plastics Research and Development Company:*
PRADCO
P.O. Box 1587
Fort Smith, AR 72902
800-531-1201

Zephyr Services offers a computer program for IBM compatible computers which gives the time and height in feet and inches for high and low tides anywhere in Florida. Programs are also available for other states and by regions (e.g., Gulf Coast). Each program covers two years, and new programs are issued each December.
Zephyr Services
1900 Murray Avenue
Pittsburg, PA 15217
800-533-6666 or 412-422-6600

Books and Such

Any of the following books and publications will be helpful to newcomers to Florida fishing or to flats fishing in general.

Florida Sportsman magazine: There's probably no better way to keep abreast of what's happening than reading this publication on a regular basis. For less than twenty bucks a year, you'll get many well written and timely articles each month.
Subscription Service Dept.
Florida Sportsman
P.O. Box 59200
Boulder, CO 80322-9200

Choosing and Using Knots, from Stren Line, is a newly revised booklet edited by Lefty Kreh that includes mention of the new braided lines. To get a copy, send $2.95 ($3.50 Can.) to:
Stren Knot Book Offer
Stren Fishing Lines
Delle Donne Corporate Center,
1011 Centre Road
Wilmington, DL 19805-1270
800-243-9700
CIS 73150,543

Fishing Lines, available from Florida DER. This booklet lists a great deal of information concerning species found in all Florida waters, including physical descriptions and color pictures for identification. It also includes information on licenses, other regulations, closed seasons and bag and size limits.

Fishing the Everglades, by John Kumiski, Argonaut Publishing Co., P.O. Box 940153, Maitland, FL 32730, 407-834-2954, CIS 73742,100

Fishing the Flats, by Sosin & Kreh (Lyons & Burford, NY).

Florida Boater's Guide, available from Florida Marine Patrol.

Fly Fishing in Salt Water, by Lefty Kreh, (Lyons & Burford, NY).

Flyrodding Florida Salt, by John Kumiski, See above to order.

Modern Saltwater Fishing Tackle, by Frank T. Moss, International Marine Publishing Company.

The Redfish Book, The Snook Book, The Tarpon Book, The Trout Book, Secret Spots, Tampa Bay/Cedar Key, Secret Spots, SW Florida, Frank Sargeant. These books are available individually at $12.45 or a set of the first four for $37.95. All prices include shipping and handling. To order write:
Larsen's Outdoor Publishing
Dept. RGS
2640 Elizabeth Place
Lakeland, FL 33813
813-644-3381

A Practical Guide To Outdoor Protection, available through The Sawyer Company. Covers protection from sun as well as insects. An excellent book, small enough to fit in a pocket or tackle box. Call 1-800-940-4464

Glossary

Apron—A structure at the base or "foot" of a bridge or spillway, usually fan-shaped and usually concrete, although it can be of wood, especially on older bridges. It's often possible to walk under a bridge on its apron.

Attractant—A material spread in the water (such as chum) or placed on a lure, and intended to literally attract fish toward an angler.

Chum—A mixture of ground fish, blood, oils and a material such as bread or soy cake put into the water and on its surface to lure game fish and the small fish on which they prey.

Copepods—Small, usually microscopic, crustaceans found in a marine environment. They are heavily grazed on by many species of fish and other marine animals, especially by filter feeders such as corals and some surprisingly large animals.

Daisy chain—A phrase used to describe the action of tarpon when they circle single file at the surface.

Detritus—Accumulated rotting debris such as leaves, dead sea grasses, etc., in the water.

Enhancer—A chemical compound used to encourage a fish to bite a lure after the fish has been attracted to and found the lure. An enhancer may be something placed on one of the hooks on a lure or a liquid or paste spread on the lure itself.

Eutrophication—The act of a body of water losing oxygen, especially to the point of being unable to support life.

Eddy (eddies)—A current running against the direction of the main current, especially in a circular motion. While they can be strong, and can represent a danger, eddies are generally slower moving than rips (q.v.). Eddies are quite apparent, for example, on the down current side of bridge pilings, jetties, and other obstructions to the tidal flow or a current.

Fish-finder rig—A device that attaches a sinker to the line using a swivel or other device which allows the line to slip freely through it.

Grains—A spear or harpoon with two or more barbed prongs used in the taking of fish.

Hypothermia—Extreme lowering of body temperature due to cold, frequently found in people who have been in water for long periods of time. Can be life-threatening.

ICW—The Intracoastal Waterway, by which a boat can travel the length of the east coast and around Florida into the Gulf states without going into the open ocean.

IGFA—The International Game Fish Association, the organization that recognizes and tracks record fish, and works to promote conservation and sport fishing.

Jig (noun)—A lure with a heavy metal head and one hook, which usually points upward, and a dressing of some type that flows around the body of the hook, giving the hook the appearance of a body. The dressing may be a man-made material, feathers, animal hair or plastic. Some jigs, intended to be fished straight down, called "diamond jigs," are shaped as a diamond in cross section and usually have a treble hook.

Jig (verb)—The act of giving a lure action by means of moving the rod tip in an up-and-down motion. Almost any lure can be "jigged."

Littoral current—A current which runs parallel to the shore, as does the current which runs down the eastern coast of the United States.

Pelagic—Marine life living in the open seas as opposed to inshore or nearshore waters.

Pharyngeal teeth—Teeth located far back in the throat, in the area of the pharynx. Sometimes called "crushers," these are sturdy teeth which can pulverize shells of clams, crabs and often even oysters.

Plankton—Plant and animal life that drift at the mercy of wind and current, especially on the open seas. From the Greek word for "wanderer."

Plug (noun)—An artificial lure made to resemble a bait fish and given a swimming or struggling action by the angler. Plugs got their name from the plug of wood from which the early models were carved, but are today more often made of strong plastic.

Plug (verb)—A means of taking fish, as in "we're going to be plugging for tarpon today." The implication is plugs will be used as opposed to live or dead bait, or another type of artificial lure other than plugs.

Pneumatophores—A specialized, upward-growing root found in certain aquatic plants such as the mangrove and cypress trees, through which respiratory gas exchanges occur, often needed because of a lack of oxygen in the mud or soil in which the tree is rooted.

Rip—A current disturbed by an opposing current or by passage over or around obstructions or passing over an uneven or obstructed bottom. Unlike eddies (q.v.), rip "tides" or rip currents (generally called simply a "rip") are frequently quite swift, and are sometimes the cause of swimmers drowning.

Spoon—An artificial lure resembling the business end of an eating spoon, somewhat elongated and having a hook, usually a treble hook, but sometimes a single hook, at one end and a line attachment point at the other. Spoons can be cast or trolled, and are most effective when retrieved slowly.

Tin squids—A metal lure in various shapes, often with a highly polished and shiny finish. Many resemble the handle of a dinner knife and, in fact, such handles were cut and drilled for the specific purpose of use as a lure. The well known Hopkins tins evolved from the knife handle tin. The origin of the word "tin" comes from the metal originally used to mold lures, although most tin squids in use today are plated metal. (The Hopkins lures are a notable exception and are solid stainless

steel.) Squids generally have only one hook, at the rear, sometimes single, usually a treble hook.

Wash—That portion of water at the beach from the area of the
last breaking wave to the highest point the water reaches on a
beach and generally full of foam.

White Bait—Any of a number of small baitfish, such as but not
limited to; greenback minnows (greenies), grunts, mutton minnows, pigfish, and sardines.

Index

C

D

E

F